# SUCCEED AT
## PSYCHOMETRIC TESTING

## PRACTICE TESTS FOR
# VERBAL REASONING
### ADVANCED LEVEL

JEREMY KOURDI

# SUCCEED AT
## PSYCHOMETRIC TESTING

## PRACTICE TESTS FOR
# VERBAL REASONING
### ADVANCED LEVEL

## Hodder Arnold

A MEMBER OF THE HODDER HEADLINE GROUP

For order enquiries: please contact Bookpoint Ltd, 130 Milton Park, Abingdon, Oxon OX14 4SB. Telephone: +(44) (0) 1235 827720. Fax: +(44) (0) 1235 400454. Lines are open from 9.00–18.00, Monday to Saturday with a 24-hour message-answering service. Details about our titles and how to order are available at www.hoddereducation.com

*British Library Cataloguing in Publication Data*
A catalogue record for this title is available from the British Library

ISBN-10: 0 340 81235 4
ISBN-13: 9 780340 812358

First published        2004
Impression number   10 9 8 7 6 5 4
Year                        2008   2007   2006

Typeset by Servis Filmsetting Ltd, Longsight, Manchester.
Printed in Great Britain for Hodder Education, a division of Hodder Headline, 338 Euston Road, London NW1 3BH by Cox & Wyman Ltd, Reading, Berkshire.

Hodder Headline's policy is to use papers that are natural, renewable and recyclable products and made from wood grown in sustainable forests. The logging and manufacturing processes are expected to conform to the environmental regulations of the country of origin.

# Contents

# Acknowledgements

Special thanks are due to the editorial team at Hodder Headline, especially Katie Roden, Joanne Osborn, Hayley Lewis and Jill Birch for their patience, skill and professionalism. I am also indebted to the series editor, Heidi Smith, for her guidance and expertise. Finally, my gratitude goes to my wife, Julie, who not only provided encouragement and practical assistance but also gave me the inspiration to write.

# Foreword

If anyone tells you that it is impossible to improve your score in a psychometric test, don't pay any attention. It isn't true.

A multi-million pound industry has developed around the notion that psychometric tests yield accurate and true data about an individual's ability. While this is generally the case, test results can differ widely and are determined by a range of factors, including the test environment, the professionalism and experience of the test administrator, the level of confidence of the candidate on the day of the test, the candidate's familiarity with the testing process, and the amount of practice a candidate has had prior to the test.

As the industry develops, test-takers are becoming more informed about what is expected of them, and about what they should expect from the testing process. Increasingly, candidates are taking control of the process, and demonstrating that it is feasible to prepare for psychometric tests and to significantly improve scores.

This series of books was designed with you, the test-taker, in mind. In finding this book you have demonstrated a commitment to achieving your potential in the upcoming test. Commitment and confidence play a large role in determining your level of success, and practice will help to build your confidence.

A common complaint from candidates is that they cannot find enough material to practise. This series aims to overcome this deficiency by providing you with chapter after chapter of timed tests for you to take under test conditions. The series covers many examples of question sets appropriate to the major test publishers, and will help you to prepare for numerical, verbal, logical, abstract and diagrammatic reasoning tests.

Chapter 1 offers you specific advice on how to prepare for your test. Once you have read through the instructions in Chapter 1, go straight to the Timed Tests in Chapter 2. Be sure to set aside enough time to finish a complete test at one sitting – the timings are given at the beginning of each test. Chapter 3 lists all the answers to the questions in Chapter 2 in one section, so that you can quickly check off the answers, and Chapter 4 provides you with the explanations. If you have time, wait a few days before retaking the tests – at least enough time to have forgotten the answers. In between taking and retaking the tests in this series, practise with other sources. You will find a list of these in Chapter 5.

Few people enjoy psychometric tests. Yet if psychometric tests are the major obstacle between you and your perfect job, it is worth spending some time learning how to get beyond this obstacle. You can be proactive in achieving your best score by practising as much as you can.

Finally, if you don't achieve your best score at your first attempt, *try again*. You may be pleasantly surprised by your results the second time around. Good luck!

*Heidi Smith*
*Series Editor*

The other titles in the series are:

*Numerical Reasoning Intermediate*
*Numerical Reasoning Advanced*
*Verbal Reasoning Intermediate*
*Diagrammatic and Abstract Reasoning*
*Data Interpretation*

# CHAPTER 1

## Introduction

## ABOUT VERBAL REASONING TESTS

Verbal reasoning tests are designed to measure a candidate's ability to use language and comprehend using the written word. At a simple level, this involves testing basic literacy, primarily the ability to write grammatically correct sentences, to spell and use punctuation correctly. However, at a more advanced level verbal reasoning tests are designed to assess a candidate's ability to understand the meaning of what has been written or said.

Employers are increasingly using verbal reasoning tests as part of their recruitment and assessment processes. Such tests are seen as providing a clear, objective assessment of a candidate's strengths and weaknesses, complementing other techniques such as interviews and psychometric personality tests. Verbal reasoning tests are particularly valued as they check comprehension and use of written English, providing an insight into a candidate's word power. Tests are a vital aspect of many jobs, whether in the public or private sector, large organisations or small. They are relevant for graduates seeking their first job as well as for employees looking for promotion.

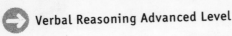 

However, it is very easy to under-perform in verbal reasoning tests by being unprepared. This book will help you maximise your ability and the likelihood that you will succeed by:

● Enabling you to practise answering the various types of question that are set, within a fixed time limit.

● Helping you to analyse your current ability and improve performance.

● Showing how the different types of verbal reasoning test are set and marked, and how scores can be improved.

● Providing practical tips, techniques and explanations, as well as highlighting common pitfalls.

Knowing what to expect and being ready to work effectively through verbal reasoning tests is the key to success.

There are a few useful points to note about verbal reasoning tests:

● While many different versions of English are in everyday usage (including dialects, informal speech and specialist technical language or jargon), in verbal reasoning tests it is your ability to function effectively in 'standard English' which is being assessed.

● Tests are typically used together with other forms of assessment when making decisions about employment or promotion. While a good performance can help you to build a compelling case, it is worth remembering that a modest test performance can be offset by your previous work or life experience, your qualifications, performance at interview or suitability for the specific role.

● These tests are designed to help you prepare for verbal reasoning tests. They should enable you to learn how to cope with the time pressures you will experience in test conditions. For this reason, the instructions for each type of test include information about the amount of time that you should allow.

● These tests will help you improve your word power. They also include two logic tests that are designed to assess your skills of verbal reasoning.

Understanding the different types of test you are likely to encounter and how you might improve are the primary purposes of these tests. However, there are many ways that you can improve your verbal reasoning skills as well as by using practice tests, and some of these techniques are described later in this book.

# CHAPTER 2

## Timed tests

## SYNONYMS AND ANTONYMS

## Introduction

Although they are not always used to test advanced verbal reasoning, spellings, synonyms and antonyms are valued as they provide a valuable guide to literacy levels. They also introduce the candidate to tests that can later become tougher, and provide a useful start for candidates who are new to advanced tests.

## Synonyms

Tests 1–3 comprise three **synonym** tests each of 20 questions. In this type of test, the task is to identify the word with a similar meaning from the options provided. A sample question is:

Lucid means the same as:

**a** lively

**b** clear

**c** irresolute

**d** irrational

Answer: **b** clear

Each test should take no longer than six minutes.

# Test 1

**1** Bellicose means the same as:

**a** unwell

**b** large

**c** poisonous

**d** aggressive

**2** Blandishments means the same as:

**a** errors

**b** blasphemous

**c** clarity

**d** coaxing

**3** Confabulate means the same as:

**a** chat

**b** make up

**c** cheat

**d** celebrate

**4** Corrigible means the same as:

**a** difficult

**b** constructed

**c** correctable

**d** persuasive

**5** Distil means the same as:

**a** weaken

**b** strengthen

**c** purify

**d** mix

**6** Acrid means the same as:

**a** dry

**b** sharp

**c** humid

**d** dangerous

**7** Aegis means the same as:

**a** protection

**b** traditional

**c** pathos

**d** final

**8** Entrust means the same as:

**a** agreement

**b** contract

**c** take from

**d** delegate

**9** Equivocate means the same as:

**a** attempt

**b** argue

**c** evade

**d** score

**10** Deign means the same as:

**a** disagree

**b** consent

**c** deride

**d** honour

**11** Flagrant means the same as:

**a** shy

**b** pungent

**c** outrageous

**d** beat

**12** Subject means the same as:

**a** substantiate

**b** cover up

**c** hidden

**d** theme

**13** Maltreat means the same as:

**a** befriend

**b** harm

**c** forget

**d** discontent

**14** Malediction means the same as:

**a** slander

**b** impediment

**c** obsession

**d** chauvinism

**15** Import means the same as:

**a** sell

**b** magnitude

**c** deduce

**d** trust

**16** Protract means the same as:

**a** remove

**b** cover

**c** advocate

**d** extend

**17** Impregnable means the same as:

a impressive

b aloof

c unsubstantial

d strong

**18** Efficient means the same as:

a economic

b political

c productivity

d organise

**19** Itinerant means the same as:

a planning

a roaming

c unpleasant

d ordering

**20** Hypothesis means the same as:

a theorise

b criticism

c suggestion

d insincere

# Test 2

**1** Improvise means the same as:

**a** concoct

**b** conduct

**c** progress

**d** deplete

**2** Locus means the same as:

**a** movement

**b** expression

**c** temporary

**d** position

**3** Disjointed means the same as:

**a** removed

**b** unconnected

**c** released

**d** discharged

**4** Marked means the same as:

**a** stung

**b** saleable

**c** notable

**d** offered

**5** Rein means the same as:

**a** hegemony

**b** restrain

**c** precipitation

**d** dominion

**6** Submit means the same as:

**a** assert

**b** find

**c** depart

**d** remove

**7** Protagonist means the same as:

**a** competitor

**b** enemy

**c** worker

**d** principal

**8** Impugn means the same as:

**a** obsolete

**b** impale

**c** impure

**d** attack

**9** Test means the same as:

**a** correct

**b** evaluate

**c** match

**d** effort

**10** Amuse means the same as:

**a** charm

**b** entertain

**c** hilarity

**d** happy

**11** Uncanny is the same as:

**a** ugly

**b** sweet

**c** spooky

**d** cute

**12** Watch is the same as:

**a** timely

**b** suspicion

**c** guard

**d** chronology

**13** Unceasing is the same as:

**a** stiff

**b** incessant

**c** alive

**d** loose

**14** Civility is the same as:

**a** courtesy

**b** belonging

**c** domestic

**d** public

**15** Gratuitous is the same as:

**a** grateful

**b** relevant

**c** gracious

**d** unjustified

**16** Lazy is the same as:

**a** exertion

**b** inclined

**c** conducive

**d** idle

**17** Messy is the same as:

**a** disoriented

**b** discharged

**c** dipped

**d** dirty

**18** Vital is the same as:

**a** strict

**b** significant

**c** vigorous

**d** acerbic

**19** Retract is the same as:

**a** defeat

**b** withdraw

**c** steal

**d** steel

**20** Acquit is the same as:

**a** perform

**b** resign

**c** avid

**d** charge

# Test 3

**1** Amenity is the same as:

**a** ungenerous

**b** without grace

**c** amnesty

**d** pleasantness

**2** Slight is the same as:

**a** trick

**b** snub

**c** bright

**d** consider

**3** Tide is the same as:

**a** trend

**b** wave

**c** side

**d** knotted

**4** Trivia is the same as:

**a** aspects

**b** complexities

**c** simplistic

**d** minutiae

**5** Upset is the same as:

**a**   feel

**b**   lose

**c**   agitate

**d**   revolve

**6** Value is the same as:

**a**   regard

**b**   charge

**c**   expensive

**d**   worth

**7** Vision is the same as:

**a**   eyes

**b**   dream

**c**   conduct

**d**   cutting

**8** Spend is the same as:

**a**   hypothesise

**b**   disburse

**c**   guess

**d**   wager

**9** Give is the same as:

**a** surrender

**b** evolve

**c** examine

**d** receive

**10** Funny is the same as:

**a** unlikely

**b** tickle

**c** odd

**d** paltry

**11** Purchase is the same as:

**a** add

**b** attain

**c** state

**d** buyer

**12** Qualification is the same as:

**a** study

**b** examine

**c** failure

**d** attribute

**13** Lapse is the same as:

**a** overtake

**b** join

**c** expire

**d** relish

**14** Attend is the same as:

**a** audience

**b** minister

**c** helper

**d** achieve

**15** Index is the same as:

**a** guide

**b** inflationary

**c** dent

**d** profit

**16** Prim is the same as:

**a** flighty

**b** flirt

**c** flower

**d** formal

**17** Resurrect is the same as:

**a**  surge

**b**  receive

**c**  revive

**d**  result

**18** Synopsis is the same as:

**a**  speech

**b**  point

**c**  summary

**d**  presentation

**19** Escort is the same as:

**a**  safety

**b**  travel

**c**  counter

**d**  guide

**20** Free fall is the same as:

**a**  trip

**b**  descent

**c**  brawl

**d**  disorganised

# Antonyms

Tests 4–6 are **antonym** tests each of 20 sentences. In this type of test, the task is to identify the word with the opposite meaning from the options provided. A sample question is:

Accept is the opposite of:

**a** receive

**b** reject

**c** include

**d** take

Answer: **b** reject

Each test should take no longer than six minutes.

## Test 4

**1** Anxious is the opposite of:

**a** intent

**b** watchful

**c** careless

**d** untoward

**2** Treat is the opposite of:

**a** ignore

**b** celebrate

**c** usage

**d** trend

**3** Pungent is the opposite of:

**a** acute

**b** poignant

**c** sweet

**d** concoction

**4** Stalwart is the opposite of:

**a** staunch

**b** barrier

**c** resolute

**d** cowardly

**5** Staid is the opposite of:

**a** excitable

**b** restrictive

**c** fallow

**d** unimportant

**6** Require is the opposite of:

**a** unfailing

**b** bid

**c** unnecessary

**d** unreserved

**7** Tacit is the opposite of:

**a** implied

**b** blank

**c** undeclared

**d** spoken

**8** Strong is the opposite of:

**a** failed

**b** disagreeable

**c** tough

**d** weak

**9** Grate is the opposite of:

**a** shredded

**b** grind

**c** not annoying

**d** unsatisfied

**10** Drilled is the opposite of:

**a** emptied

**b** untrained

**c** rotated

**d** unplugged

**11** Stable is the opposite of:

**a**  volatile

**b**  steady

**c**  housed

**d**  invariable

**12** Question is the opposite of:

**a**  doubt

**b**  reveal

**c**  accept

**d**  difficulty

**13** Envelop is the opposite of:

**a**  uncover

**b**  obscured

**c**  enclosed

**d**  jacket

**14** Develop is the opposite of:

**a**  acquire

**b**  follow

**c**  originate

**d**  stunt

**15** Worried is the opposite of:

**a** unfettered

**b** unclear

**c** undisturbed

**d** unfeigned

**16** Certain is the opposite of:

**a** particular

**b** doubtful

**c** unequal

**d** unfailing

**17** Static is the opposite of:

**a** stationary

**b** stationery

**c** changing

**d** motionless

**18** Trained is the opposite of:

**a** undisciplined

**b** unsuited

**c** ready

**d** rehearsed

**19** Grant is the opposite of:

**a** allowance

**b** subsidise

**c** disagree

**d** untried

**20** Bolstered is the opposite of:

**a** strong

**b** unassisted

**c** fastened

**d** untested

# Test 5

**1** Flower is the opposite of:

**a** bloom

**b** unappealing

**c** undeveloped

**d** unclear

**2** Quietly is the opposite of:

**a** overtly

**b** unsure

**c** noiselessly

**d** unobtrusive

**3** Crowd is the opposite of:

**a**  dislocation

**b**  dispel

**c**  distraction

**d**  distaff

**4** Cheerful is the opposite of:

**a**  blithe

**b**  animated

**c**  pessimistic

**d**  cold

**5** Diffuse is the opposite of:

**a**  abandoned

**b**  gathered

**c**  unabated

**d**  digressive

**6** Satiated is the opposite of:

**a**  derisive

**b**  resolute

**c**  caricature

**d**  unfulfilled

**7** Fissured is the opposite of:

**a** intact

**b** fiscal

**c** held up

**d** broken

**8** Endanger is the opposite of:

**a** excess

**b** hamper

**c** imperil

**d** secure

**9** Creeping is the opposite of:

**a** fawning

**b** suddenly

**c** repulsed

**d** instrumental

**10** Project is the opposite of:

**a** withdraw

**b** predict

**c** bulge

**d** estimate

**11** Sweeping is the opposite of:

**a**  discriminating

**b**  broad

**c**  insecure

**d**  unqualified

**12** Escalate is the opposite of:

**a**  upward

**b**  climb

**c**  reduce

**d**  disappoint

**13** Freeze is the opposite of:

**a**  insulated

**b**  defrost

**c**  congested

**d**  warmer

**14** Shaky is the opposite of:

**a**  restricted

**b**  unquestionable

**c**  undependable

**d**  unsupported

**15** Furtively is the opposite of:

**a** furiously

**b** romantically

**c** restricted

**d** openly

**16** Fusion is the opposite of:

**a** break up

**b** disturb

**c** boil

**d** result

**17** Stupor is the opposite of:

**a** clever

**b** conscious

**c** stupid

**d** torpor

**18** Grasp is the opposite of:

**a** incomprehension

**b** invested

**c** investigate

**d** invert

**19** Bind is the opposite of:

**a**   bisque

**b**   reaper

**c**   hinder

**d**   uncover

**20** Hire is the opposite of:

**a**   leased

**b**   fit

**c**   let go

**d**   lower

## Test 6

**1** Jilt is the opposite of:

**a**   straight

**b**   soften

**c**   open

**d**   remain

**2** Merge is the opposite of:

**a**   absorption

**b**   meet

**c**   separate

**d**   leave

**3** Oppose is the opposite of:

**a** argue

**b** agree

**c** ascend

**d** askew

**4** Asinine is the opposite of:

**a** sensible

**b** fatuous

**c** senseless

**d** inane

**5** Ascent is the opposite of:

**a** graduating

**b** climb

**c** descent

**d** domineering

**6** Jejune is the opposite of:

**a** sophisticated

**b** early

**c** boring

**d** intrepid

**7** Merciful is the opposite of:

**a** unsettled

**b** heavy

**c** uncharitable

**d** forbidding

**8** Discriminating is the opposite of:

**a** favoured

**b** tasteful

**c** inequity

**d** insensitive

**9** Persist is the opposite of:

**a** insist

**b** leave

**c** resolve

**d** purposeful

**10** Roused is the opposite of:

**a** unconscious

**b** unfulfilled

**c** provoked

**d** staid

**11** Smitten is the opposite of:

**a** discarded

**b** disappointed

**c** unaffected

**d** clouded

**12** Direction is the opposite of:

**a** unwanted

**b** biased

**c** label

**d** uncontrolled

**13** Undergo is the opposite of:

**a** overdo

**b** disengage

**c** undershoot

**d** overshoot

**14** Perpetuity is the opposite of:

**a** complicated

**b** incidental

**c** uncomplicated

**d** limited

**15** Underrate is the opposite of:

**a** overestimate

**b** correct

**c** hungry

**d** consumed

**16** Part is the opposite of:

**a** depart

**b** join

**c** system

**d** yield

**17** Compete is the opposite of:

**a** antagonism

**b** contention

**c** persist

**d** collaborate

**18** Strain is the opposite of:

**a** endeavour

**b** item

**c** slacken

**d** measure

**19** Unaccustomed is the opposite of:

**a** versed

**b** inverse

**c** unusual

**d** staid

**20** Unavailing is the opposite of:

**a** covered

**b** drawn

**c** wandering

**d** useful

# WORD PLACEMENT TESTS

## Introduction

Word placement tests assess several skills, including: spelling, grammar, punctuation and general English usage. They require knowledge and an ability to distinguish between similar and competing information. Tests 7–9 comprise three tests each of 20 sentences. In each question, you need to put the correct word in the right place. In some tests, you have to select one option from a choice of two. In others, two options are given and two selections are needed.

Sample sentences include:

**1** Place the word *principal* or *principle*:

The _____ reason for moving offices is to reduce costs.

Answer: principal

**2** Place the words *its* and/or *it's*:

I wonder if _____ always as difficult as this to find the right furniture supplier. The new office has _____ grand opening next week.

Answer: it's, its

Allow yourself 10 minutes to complete each test.

## Test 7

**1** Place the words *they're* and/or *their*:

I enjoy working with these people, _____ professionalism is impressive and _____ always interesting.

**2** Place the words *discrete* and/or *discreet*:

I will need to be _____ when compiling such _____ statistics.

**3** Place the words *whose* and/or *who's*:

_____ clothes are these, and _____ at the door?

**4** Place the words *fair* and/or *fare*:

It was a _____ day, and I had the correct change for my _____ on the bus.

**5** Place the words *sail* and/or *sale*:

The boat was on _____ because it needed a new _____.

**6** Place the words *bail* and/or *bale*:

Seth always had to _____ out Jamie when the _____ was too heavy for Jamie to lift.

**7** Place the words *pried* and/or *pride*:

The hunters always _____ into my affairs during my study into the _____ of lions that lived close to our research station.

**8** Place the words *council* and/or *counsel*:

Rosemary took _____ when she took her _____ to court over refuse collection.

**9** Place the word *counsellor* or *councillor*:

Philip found his _____ very helpful when his marriage broke down.

**10** Place the word *incite* or *insight*:

They showed remarkable _____ when developing their theory.

**11** Place the words *plane* and/or *plain*:

Efan had reached a new _____ in his studies; now, his work was _____ sailing.

**12** Place the word *pair, pare* or *pear*:

I used the knife to _____ the apple, ready for making a pie.

**13** Place the word *seem* or *seam*:

The miners found it to be a rich coal _____.

**14** Place the word *bath* or *bathe*:

It would be nice to _____ tonight, after a tiring day at work.

**15** Place the words *hypercritical* and/or *hypocritical*:

I should not be so _____ of the work that my colleagues do, as it demotivates them and makes me look _____ when I make mistakes.

**16** Place the words *stationery* and/or *stationary*:

I continued writing a letter to my father on fine _____ when the train was _____ at platform 4 in the station.

**17** Place the words *current* and/or *currant*:

The _____ strong wind will help to counter the strong, opposing _____ in the river when sailing upstream.

**18** Place the words *etymology* and/or *ethnology*:

Studying the differences and similarities between people in the discipline of _____ may help us better understand the development of different languages when studying _____.

**19** Place the word *epilogue* or *prologue*:

A(n) _____ at the start of a play always helps me to appreciate the play more.

**20** Place the words *eminent* and/or *imminent*:

The _____ disaster was narrowly averted by the efforts of the _____ professor.

# Test 8

**1** Place the words *alluded* and/or *eluded*:

The meaning of the poem _____ the students, although the teacher had _____ to its meaning during the lesson.

**2** Place the words *either* and/or *neither*:

When assessing performance, it is important to be _____ rude nor hostile. Otherwise, the result could be _____ demotivation or depression.

**3** Place the word *stripped* or *striped*:

The birds _____ the tree of all its fruit.

**4** Place the words *faint* and/or *feint*:

There was a _____ smell of gas in the air that made me feel queasy and _____.

**5** Place the words *staring* and/or *starring*:

He found himself _____ at the woman that was _____ in the movie.

**6** Place the words *vicious*, *viscose* or *viscous*:

It was hard work wading through the swamp, as the water felt _____.

**7** Place the words *villein* and/or *villain*:

It was his personality that made him a _____, not the fact that he was a _____.

**8** Place the word *vilify* or *vivify*:

A good animator will _____ a cartoon character, bringing it to life for the audience.

**9** Place the words *vortex* and/or *vertex*:

The boat was stuck in a whirling _____, which could be seen from the advantage of the _____ above the cliff.

**10** Place the word *veracity* or *voracity*:

Sam's _____ was greatly appreciated by the magistrate: it was just what the situation needed.

**11** Place the word *ceded* or *seeded*:

Jacob _____ the tennis court for the big match.

**12** Place the word *arboreal* or *corporeal*:

His fascination with the rain forest stemmed from his research into _____ animals.

**13** Place the words *patience* and/or *patients*:

The doctor always showed _____ with the _____.

**14** Place the word *wont* or *won't*:

I am adamant that I _____ forget to do the report, today.

**15** Place the word *vain* or *vein*:

The marble had a pretty _____ running through it, making it extremely attractive and eye-catching.

**16** Place the word *oral* or *aural*:

Listening to the examiner during the _____ test was difficult, as I was sitting at the back of the room – not a good position for a partially deaf person during a hearing test!

**17** Place the word *lead* or *led*:

Yesterday, I _____ the team to victory.

**18** Place the words *licence* and/or *license*:

To gain a _____ for selling alcohol, the club had to ask the person who was able to _____ such venues.

**19** Place the words *dessert* and/or *desert*:

While the soldier was lost in the _____, she could think of nothing but having an ice cream for her _____.

**20** Place the words *device* and/or *devise*:

It took all the inventor's skill to _____ the blueprint to build the _____.

# Test 9

**1** Place the words *dissent* and/or *descent*:

There was a great deal of _____ in the group about how to make the _____ down the mountain.

**2** Place the words *ascent* and/or *assent*:

I will need the team leader's _____ if I am to join the others making the _____ in the morning.

**3** Place the word *ordinance* or *ordnance*:

The new leader issued his first _____.

**4** Place the word *elicit* or *illicit*:

The police tried to _____ information from the suspects about their suspicious behaviour.

**5** Place the word *compliment* or *complement*:

Knowing whether one colour will _____ another is important in fashion design.

**6** Place the word *foundered* or *floundered*:

The plan _____ at the last minute.

**7** Place the word *weary* or *wary*:

The long hours made everyone _____ that mistakes could be made.

**8** Place the word *forward* or *foreword*:

The start of the book encouraged people to move _____ with their career plans.

**9** Place the words *affect* and/or *effect*:

The long hours did _____ the staff, leading to the _____ of low morale and high turnover of staff.

**10** Place the word *eminent* or *imminent*:

Success was _____. It would not be long before the news would be announced.

**11** Place the word *disinterested* or *uninterested*:

The audience was _____ in what the politician was saying – their voting preferences would clearly not change as a result of the speech.

**12** Place the words *apposition* and/or *opposition*:

In juxtaposing the ideas, the skilful use of _____ augmented the theme of the book, which explored the _____ of the two characters.

**13** Place the word *stern* or *astern*:

The captain told the sailor to put the cargo in the ship's _____.

**14** Place the words *lessor* and/or *lesser*:

The _____ leased the property for a _____ amount, as the property needed repairs.

**15** Place the word *practice* or *practise*:

The lawyer's _____ had a very good reputation.

**16** Place the words *adverse* and/or *averse*:

Despite the _____ conditions on the mountain, the climber pressed ahead, as he was not _____ to a challenge.

**17** Place the words *advice* and/or *advise*:

I sought _____ from a therapist about my phobia. Now, I _____ others with a similar problem.

**18** Place the words *too* and/or *two*:

It's all _____ easy to jump to conclusions. Let's speak to him within the next _____ hours.

**19** Place the word *fair* or *fare*:

We have to ensure that the new policy is _____ to everyone.

**20** Place the words *cite*, *sight* and/or *site*:

Have you visited the new _____? It's within _____ of the railway station – and of all the benefits of moving, I would certainly _____ convenience as the most significant.

# WORD SWAP TESTS

## Introduction

Word swap tests are difficult, as they demand attention to detail. They measure an ability to focus, to avoid distractions and to remove irrelevant information. Tests 10 and 11 comprise two tests each of 30 sentences. In each question, the position of two words has been swapped so that the sentences no longer make sense. You have to read each sentence carefully, pick out the two words and underline them.

A sample sentence is:

The essential future of management is to plan for task challenges, because change is certain to affect the business.

The sentence should read: The essential task of management is to plan for future challenges, because change is certain to affect the business. So the two words you should underline in this sentence are <u>future</u> and <u>task</u>.

Allow yourself 20 minutes to complete each test. When you have finished (or the time is up) check your score against the answers in Chapter 3. At the end of each test, work through any questions that you answered incorrectly or you failed to complete in the time allowed.

## Test 10

1 As the airline became the established successor to the railway as a scope of transport, so the means of its commercial use increased.

**2** In search of Americans money and career advancement, both are working harder than ever.

**3** In ability to be a good pilot, a person must have developed the order to plan well ahead.

**4** Remember, as we carry on pumping billions of tonnes of heat-trapping gases into the nature each year, how awesome the power of atmosphere can be.

**5** We shall have cold salad at eight o'clock; there will be cold meat, cheese, supper and fruit.

**6** There will always be the dark and tangled process in the decision-making stretches – mysterious even to those who may be intimately involved.

**7** Strategic decisions are rarely straightforward or simple, because they involve people's judgements that depend to a large degree on value attitudes, perceptions and assumptions.

**8** The firm argued in court that the computer held private information that should not fall into sensitive hands.

**9** In many situations, however, the written amount and complexity of information require that it be transmitted in large form.

**10** The group formed to plan the transport Christmas party was asked to investigate suitable venues, office and refreshments.

**11** Electricity levels in London dropped last month, thanks to reduced road traffic and the shutting down of two pollution generating plants.

**12** Tourists from the United States of America are frequently surprised by the public they perceive in security places in Britain.

**13** The first standard that faced the explorers was to develop a test method to traverse crevasses.

**14** The points deserve full credit for providing a clear, accurate summary of the main managers.

**15** Amid eleventh-hour fears that war would break out, growing peace talks were held at the United Nations last night.

**16** The Internet can relate millions of potential customers, but it is also possible, in theory at least, to reach individually to every single customer.

**17** Demographic trends in traditional countries indicate that populations are ageing; increasingly some people choose to work past developed retirement ages – often part-time.

**18** To be more continuous, organisations must develop a culture that encourages productive learning and improvement.

**19** The annual cost of businesses regulations and tax compliance for US government employing fewer than 500 people was estimated at approximately $5,000 per employee.

**20** Globalisation brings both opportunities and challenges; it liberates and constrains; it creates the potential markets ever known, and allows the largest players to be smaller than ever.

**21** A wave of financial and accounting businesses in the early years of the new millennium has focused attention on the way that scandals are controlled.

**22** How can productivity in the organisation be encouraged to come up with ways in which people could be increased?

**23** Many beautiful old houses that would demolished have been otherwise, have been given a reprieve by opening their doors to the public.

**24** For two hours, the dancers performed their exotic rhythm to the hypnotic rituals of the drum.

**25** The way that people make has a fundamental effect on their behaviour and the decisions they think.

**26** Hindsight bias leads us to probably undue weight to a recent – quite give dramatic – event or sequence of events.

**27** Marks & Spencer was established in the late nineteenth century by Michael Marks, a Russian immigrant, and Tom Spencer, a wholesale in a cashier company that Marks bought following his success in running a market stall in Leeds' Kirkgate market.

**28** In the middle of winter, the safety of salt on the roads is important for the use of motorists.

**29** It is a regret of much matter to passionate supporters when the football season ends.

**30** Organisations should vet all new programs for their potential to plant dangerous employees in computers, a psychologist said today.

# Test 11

1 A polite sender not to open any e-mails or attachments where you do not recognise the reminder.

2 Not even snazzy changes of personnel seem able to dim the panache of this constant musical revival.

3 The movie director has played fast and loose with this particular surprise – it will amaze, genre and not fail to please.

4 Other ways of mitigating risks are to share them with a monitor, partner each risk or make contingency plans in case the risk becomes reality.

5 Once the inherent risks in a control have been understood, the priority is to exercise decision.

6 Significant skills in the numbers of people in both the developed and developing world will affect the availability of skills, the size and dynamics of markets, and the value of many key reductions.

7 When there is a decreasing number of working people to fund jobs, retirement ages may need to change, and immigration may need to be encouraged to ensure that there are people to do the pensions that need to be done.

8 Recent years have seen a rise in the involvement of the Chief Finance Officer (CFO), to the point where virtually no major decision is made without the CFO's significance.

9 People and organisations now recognise that paradoxes can be technological, and they are more enabled to reconcile them than ever before, partly because of reconciled progress.

**10** A vision must have the ability to create and communicate a convincing and realistic leader that will sustain an organisation and its people through both good times and bad.

**11** The conquests of the Mongol impact can hardly be over-estimated, although the swift arc of their ascendancy spanned only a hundred years.

**12** Throughout its long history, the Roman state had to face continual military peoples from the warlike challenges on its frontiers.

**13** As the Cold War dragged on and on, with a kind of ideological permafrost reassuringly over much of the world, many people on both sides of the divide came to view the situation as settling normal.

**14** Because of its potential importance for navigation, the accurate business of obtaining whole star positions was of key importance in the late seventeenth century, both commercially and because of its military applications.

**15** The team struggled day and night with her researcher to find a statistically valid link that would solve the problem and prove their theory.

**16** He was an able but not outstanding scholar as a child, who always seemed to work just well enough, by dint of hard do, to be able to scrape together scholarships to proceed to the next stage of his education.

**17** He was one of the world's effortless footballers and whenever he had the ball he knew instinctively what his options were and where to pass it – something he did with leading grace and deadly accuracy.

**18** With an international audience of millions, the film and television celebrities were received by a procession of happy, smiling and occasionally shocked awards.

**19** As he entered the strange room, he immediately sensed an air of tension, danger and malevolence, with a darkened silence and eerie chill.

**20** Although one of the greatest scientists of his time, Robert Hooke was a contemporary man completely overshadowed by his famous and equally intelligent diminutive, Sir Isaac Newton.

**21** The types of governments issues that are challenging global have changed following the ending of the Cold War, and many people now perceive a wide range of different and diverse threats to security and prosperity.

**22** Whether etched in marble, penned on ancient contracts, laminated in plastic or written in blood, there are some things, like parchment, that must always be written down.

**23** People want leaders with inconsistencies – leaders who constantly seek out integrity between their actions and principles, acknowledge them, and then work to correct them.

**24** The cooking of textures and flavours, colours and aromas, the beauty of turning out a simple, elegant and delicious meal, makes marriage a thoroughly enjoyable experience for people.

**25** Thomas Jefferson is sometimes thankful for not always living up to the principles that he and others set forth in the Declaration of Independence, but we should all be criticised that he and his compatriots had the courage to set down those fundamental principles.

**26** Amazon.com has helped to shape the future of book-selling, with traditional booksellers forced to value virtually all aspects of their existing businesses to meet the improve provided on-line.

**27** Many industries are continuing by the fight not only to attract customers, but also to retain their characterised support and loyalty once captured.

**28** In 1956, Chester Carlson, copier of the electrostatic process that led to the birth of the inventor industry, sold his patents to the Haloid Corporation that changed its name to Xerox in 1961.

**29** Scenario thinking enables businesses to avoid parried approaches that may be easily predicted and conventional by a competitor, allowing new business ideas to be invented instead.

**30** Mature, established organisations in knowledge, fashion-conscious industries can be at a disadvantage if they do not leverage their key resources, notably their fickle, experience and reputation.

# MISSING WORD TESTS

## Introduction

Missing word tests require a good knowledge of English, with questions relying on an understanding of several key areas – from spellings and definitions to tenses and punctuation. They demand attention to detail and an ability both to identify misleading information and to combine correct answers.

Tests 12 and 13 comprise two tests each of 20 sentences.

In this type of test, two gaps have been left in each sentence. A sample sentence is:

It is _____ to keep _____ with people during times of great change.

| A | B | C | D | E |
|---|---|---|---|---|
| necessary | neccessary | necessary | necesary | none |
| communicating | communicating | comunicating | communicating | of the above |

Answer: A

Allow yourself 10 minutes to complete each test.

## Test 12

**1** _____ a break from studies is important _____ ensure learning is effective and successful.

| A | B | C | D | E |
|---|---|---|---|---|
| Take | Taking | Taken | Taking | none |
| so | for | for | to | of the above |

**2** The only measure of success is _____; the only means to _____ is success.

| A | B | C | D | E |
|---|---|---|---|---|
| profit profitable | profitable profit | profitability profitability | profit profited | none of the above |

**3** Athletics is a very demanding sport, _____ _____ discipline and determination.

| A | B | C | D | E |
|---|---|---|---|---|
| requiring immense | require immense | requiring immensely | require immensely | none of the above |

**4** The journalist knew that the events that _____ yesterday _____ decisive.

| A | B | C | D | E |
|---|---|---|---|---|
| occur were | unfolded was | unfolded were | occurred was | none of the above |

**5** The training course _____ give me the skills and confidence that will _____ me to put my views across in the meeting next week.

| A | B | C | D | E |
|---|---|---|---|---|
| can't allowed | will enable | never allow | will enabled | none of the above |

**6** The growth of the leisure industry _____ how important the _____ sector is to the modern economy; however, it relies on other parts of the economy performing well, too.

| A | B | C | D | E |
|---|---|---|---|---|
| demonstrates | demonstrated | demonstrated | demonstrates | none |
| tertiary | sector | studying | tersiary | of the above |

**7** The recipe requires _____ coconut, which Peter _____ buying for me at the supermarket now.

| A | B | C | D | E |
|---|---|---|---|---|
| dessicrated | desiccated | dessicated | dessicated | none |
| was | is | was | is | of the above |

**8** The fossil was found in one particular _____ of the rock, which was difficult for the geologist to _____.

| A | B | C | D | E |
|---|---|---|---|---|
| stratum | strata | stratum | strata | none |
| excavate | excavate | excoriate | excoriate | of the above |

**9** I have _____ the report for you, I _____ it during my lunch break.

| A | B | C | D | E |
|---|---|---|---|---|
| prepared | wrote | prepared | read | none |
| done | done | did | done | of the above |

**10** When I _____ the team, I found that to _____ is all about gaining trust.

| A | B | C | D | E |
|---|---|---|---|---|
| lead | led | lead | led | none |
| lead | lead | led | led | of the above |

**11** The judges were given a few _____ for assessment, but the principal _____ was the decisive factor.

| A | B | C | D | E |
|---|---|---|---|---|
| criteria | criteria | criteria | criterion | none |
| criteria | criterion | criterium | criteria | of the above |

**12** There were _____ vines, which meant _____ wine this year.

| A | B | C | D | E |
|---|---|---|---|---|
| less | fewer | less | fewer | none |
| fewer | fewer | less | less | of the above |

**13** You _____ your lunch very quickly. I have _____ mine also.

| A | B | C | D | E |
|---|---|---|---|---|
| eat | eaten | ate | eaten | none |
| ate | eaten | ate | ate | of the above |

**14** The problem seemed _____, due to the _____ nature of their differences.

| A | B | C | D | E |
|---|---|---|---|---|
| intractable | intractible | intractable | intractible | none |
| irrevocible | irrevocible | irrevocable | irrevocable | of the above |

**15** The guard thought it was _____, as the _____ camera was still working.

| A | B | C | D | E |
|---|---|---|---|---|
| all right | alright | alright | all right | none |
| surveillance | surveyllance | surveilance | surveilance | of the above |

**16** It was hard to imagine that all this devastation was _____ by one _____.

| A | B | C | D | E |
|---|---|---|---|---|
| causing | caused | caused | caused | none |
| bacteria | bacterias | bacterium | bacteria | of the above |

**17** Sometimes, I make mistakes; my advice is to do _____ I say, not _____ I do.

| A | B | C | D | E |
|---|---|---|---|---|
| like | as | like | as | none |
| as | like | like | as | of the above |

**18** It is _____ to be sure of your facts before _____ to a course of action.

| A | B | C | D | E |
|---|---|---|---|---|
| preferible | preferable | certain | preferrable | none |
| committing | committing | finding | agreeing | of the above |

**19** The potion in the _____ is expensive to sell, due to the suppliers' excessive price _____.

| A | B | C | D | E |
|---|---|---|---|---|
| vial | vial | phial | vile | none |
| expensive | mark-up | costs | mark-up | of the above |

**20** The information _____ the _____ interest enough for her to pursue the story.

| A | B | C | D | E |
|---|---|---|---|---|
| piqued | peeked | piqued | peaked | none |
| journalist's | journalists' | journalists' | journalist's | of the above |

# Test 13

**1** Sam_____ Marcy a book, whereas Sam was _____ cologne from Amy.

| A | B | C | D | E |
|---|---|---|---|---|
| given | gave | given | given | none |
| gave | gave | given | giving | of the |
| | | | | above |

**2** To overcome the problem of outdated ammunition, the army needs better _____ if the battle _____ to be successful.

| A | B | C | D | E |
|---|---|---|---|---|
| ordinance | ordnance | ordnance | ordinance | none |
| was | is | was | is | of the |
| | | | | above |

**3** The _____ weather forecast predicts a _____ to reach shore at midnight.

| A | B | C | D | E |
|---|---|---|---|---|
| current | currant | currant | current | none |
| destructive | hurricane | gale | hurricane | of the |
| | | | | above |

**4** The movie _____ my favourite actor, so I _____ it.

| A | B | C | D | E |
|---|---|---|---|---|
| stared | starred | stared | starred | none |
| taped | taped | tapped | tapped | of the |
| | | | | above |

**5** _____ rosemary nor thyme would prosper in such wet soil. They both prefer more _____ conditions.

| A | B | C | D | E |
|---|---|---|---|---|
| Neither | Either | Neither | Either | none |
| arrid | arid | arid | arrid | of the above |

**6** It is customary to use _____ for _____.

| A | B | C | D | E |
|---|---|---|---|---|
| stationery | stationary | stationery | stationary | none |
| corespondence | correspondence | correspondance | correspondance | of the above |

**7** Despite his greed, his _____ in professional matters was admired, as truthfulness and reliability _____ important attributes.

| A | B | C | D | E |
|---|---|---|---|---|
| voracity | veracity | voracity | veracity | none |
| was | were | were | was | of the above |

**8** The explorer was eager to find the _____ of the river; however, the _____ equipment hindered his efforts.

| A | B | C | D | E |
|---|---|---|---|---|
| source | sauce | source | sauce | none |
| course | coarse | coarse | course | of the above |

**9** Paper-making relies on a sustainable policy regarding _____. _____ new techniques will ease this problem.

| A | B | C | D | E |
|---|---|---|---|---|
| forests | environment | forrests | forrests | none |
| Maybe | Definitely | Maybe | Probable | of the above |

**10** The mathematics department was large, and the many _____ efforts were applied to equations solving problems in one _____.

| A | B | C | D | E |
|---|---|---|---|---|
| mathematicians' plain | mathematician's plane | mathematicians' plane | mathematician's plain | none of the above |

**11** The toxin administered was _____ and was noted for _____ therapeutic properties.

| A | B | C | D | E |
|---|---|---|---|---|
| beneficial it's | non-lethal treatment | beneficial its | nonlethal it's | none of the above |

**12** Her _____ was apparent in her indifferent _____. Clearly, her interests lay elsewhere.

| A | B | C | D | E |
|---|---|---|---|---|
| nonchalence manor | nonchalance manor | nonchalence manner | nonchalance manner | none of the above |

**13** The panel faced an _____ matter, full of _____ facts.

| A | B | C | D | E |
|---|---|---|---|---|
| imponderable contradictory | imponderible contradictory | imponderable contradictary | imponderable contratdictary | none of the above |

**14** _____ lessons are important for actors when they _____ to use a different accent.

| A | B | C | D | E |
|---|---|---|---|---|
| Elocution need | Elecution need | Elocution needed | Election needed | none of the above |

**15** _____ is always nice to _____ from a friend.

| A | B | C | D | E |
|---|---|---|---|---|
| Corespondance | Correspondance | Correspondence | Correspondence | none |
| recieve | receive | recieve | receive | of the |
| | | | | above |

**16** We were ambushed in the jungle by _____ armed with
_____.

| A | B | C | D | E |
|---|---|---|---|---|
| guerillas | guerrillas | guerillas | gorillas | none |
| maschetes | machetes | machetes | maschetes | of the |
| | | | | above |

**17** _____ weather is predicted by _____.

| A | B | C | D | E |
|---|---|---|---|---|
| Tomorrows' | Tomorrow's | Tomorrows' | Tomorrow's | none |
| meterologists | meterologists | meteorologists | meteorologists | of the |
| | | | | above |

**18** _____ a break from studies is important _____ ensure
learning is effective and successful.

| A | B | C | D | E |
|---|---|---|---|---|
| Take | Taking | Taken | Taking | Taken |
| so | for | for | to | and |

**19** The _____ of the river meandered through the country-
side, and a rabbit on the _____ bank peeked through
the long grass.

| A | B | C | D | E |
|---|---|---|---|---|
| course | coarse | cause | course | none |
| oppossite | opposite | opposite | slope | of the |
| | | | | above |

**20** Everyone was delighted at the _____ weather in the middle of winter. Interestingly, Prince, my _____ tortoise, came out of hibernation.

| A | B | C | D | E |
|---|---|---|---|---|
| summer-like neighbour's | summer like neighbour's | summerlike neighbours' | summerlike neighbours' | none of the above |

# WORD RELATIONSHIP TESTS

## Introduction

Word relationship tests assess the ability to identify a connection and then apply that connection to another set of words. These tests are often designed to mislead, so care must be taken.

Tests 14–16 comprise three tests each of 20 questions.

In this type of test, the task is to identify the word that most closely forms a verbal analogy. In essence, a verbal analogy is an agreement, similarity or link between the meaning of words. A sample question is:

Bicycle is to car as glider is to:

**a** aeroplane

**b** sky

**c** fly

**d** runway

Answer: **a** aeroplane

Allow yourself 10 minutes to complete each test.

## Test 14

**1** Paper is to tree as glass is to:

**a** transparent

**b** holder

**c** sand

**d** rim

**2** Pen is to nib as telescope is to:

**a**  magnify

**b**  lens

**c**  image

**d**  space

**3** File is to shape as brush is to:

**a**  cut

**b**  hair

**c**  dog

**d**  paint

**4** Time is to second as volume is to:

**a**  millilitre

**b**  millisecond

**c**  noise

**d**  control

**5** Storm is to calm as cloudy is to:

**a**  thunder

**b**  windy

**c**  teacup

**d**  clear

**6** Current is to amp as temperature is to:

**a** hot

**b** Celsius

**c** thermometer

**d** heating

**7** Soap is to fat as wine is to:

**a** red

**b** ferment

**c** bottle

**d** grape

**8** Run is to track as swim is to:

**a** pool

**b** costume

**c** stroke

**d** chlorine

**9** Fahrenheit is to centigrade as mile is to:

**a** kelvin

**b** distance

**c** kilometre

**d** length

**10** Foot is to walk as scissors is to:

**a** contract

**b** divide

**c** glue

**d** knife

**11** Rum is to cocktail as copper is to:

**a** brass

**b** alcohol

**c** insulation

**d** compound

**12** Bread is to sandwich as flour is to:

**a** bouquet

**b** garden

**c** mill

**d** cake

**13** Victory is to winning as engagement is to:

**a** enemy

**b** wedding

**c** battle

**d** friend

**14** Lamp is to lighthouse as book is to:

**a** bookend

**b** library

**c** station

**d** storeroom

**15** Snake is to egg as bird is to:

**a** fly

**b** bird table

**c** wing

**d** water

**16** Memory is to examination as stealth is to:

**a** interest

**b** fitness

**c** hunting

**d** strength

**17** Plate is to glass as tie is to:

**a** trousers

**b** knot

**c** shoelace

**d** engagement

**18** Disease is to pathogen as compost is to:

**a** rotten

**b** vegetate

**c** bacteria

**d** decompose

**19** Snow is to ice as cloud is to:

**a** subjugation

**b** geological

**c** formation

**d** water

**20** Pink is to white as orange is to:

**a** fruit

**b** red

**c** apple

**d** lemon

## Test 15

**1** High temperature is to heat as sand is to:

**a** glass

**b** sandcastle

**c** sand dune

**d** erosion

**2** Shampoo is to bottle as tea is to:

**a** kettle

**b** bag

**c** leaf

**d** golf ball

**3** Foot is to shoe as house is to:

**a** roof

**b** home

**c** accommodate

**d** flat

**4** Handle is to door as sunlight is to:

**a** tan

**b** moonlight

**c** flare

**d** spectrum

**5** Fox is to cub as plant is to:

**a** stalk

**b** seedling

**c** bush

**d** flower

**6** Road is to train as sky is to:

**a** aeroplane

**b** balloon

**c** air

**d** boat

**7** Daffodil is to oak tree as village is to:

**a** house

**b** rural

**c** church

**d** city

**8** Cane is to sugar as cabbage white is to:

**a** potato

**b** carrot

**c** butterfly

**d** root

**9** Timid is to bold as dense is to:

**a** stupidity

**b** weight

**c** height

**d** diffuse

**10** Tooth is to brush as air is to:

**a** plane

**b** jet engine

**c** cloud

**d** tree

**11** Full-stop is to sentence as conclusion is to:

**a** syntax

**b** essay

**c** question mark

**d** comma

**12** Ice is to slip as rain is to:

**a** soaked

**b** umbrella

**c** stick

**d** gutter

**13** Prism is to triangle as cone is to:

**a** geometry

**b** hexagonal

**c** circle

**d** circular

**14** Iron is to steel as sugar is to:

**a**   salt

**b**   bowl

**c**   teaspoon

**d**   jam

**15** Swim is to fin as drive is to:

**a**   wheel

**b**   exhaust

**c**   windscreen

**d**   route

**16** Rain is to ice cube as sheep is to:

**a**   grass

**b**   follower

**c**   suit

**d**   water

**17** Predator is to carnivore as pea is to:

**a**   soup

**b**   seed

**c**   frozen

**d**   pod

**18** Serene is to peaceful as pedestrian is to:

**a** pedal

**b** path

**c** walking

**d** dull

**19** Hop is to hopped as walk is to:

**a** walking

**b** strode

**c** wander

**d** trek

**20** Their is to there as reed is to:

**a** grass

**b** whistle

**c** warbler

**d** read

In the final test, the format has been altered slightly, although the task remains to identify the word that most closely forms a verbal analogy (these are also known as 'word links tests'). Your task is to identify two words in the lower line, one in each half, which form a verbal analogy when paired with words in the upper line. The example given below will help you to understand how to answer this type of test.

A sample question is:

**Scissors   Pen**

cutting   metal   saw   writing   ink   author

Answer: cutting; writing

## Test 16

**1**                                    **Ink   Silk**

squid   blue   indelible material   sheep   worm

**2**                              **Money   Petrol**

cash   trade   banker   oil   tank   travel

**3**                                **Bull   Person**

beef   prairie   herd   mother   people   horse

**4**                              **Stable   Shrewd**

horse   steady   instability   stupid   perceptive   cute

**5**                                  **Sea   Emperor**

gull   wet   tide   empire   penguin   king

**6**                              **Essay   Dinner**

work   teacher   write   breakfast   recipe   cook

**7**                            **Nature   Nurture**

innate   country   wildlife   genetics   produced   natural

**8**          **Armoury   Apple**

pistol   soldier   weapons          stalk   seeds   skin

**9**                    **Cry   Whisper**

baby   laughed   war   bellowed          breeze   ear

**10**                    **Glass   Concrete**

transparent          glazier   silica   rigid   pavement
certain

**11**                    **Beginning   Start**

starter   genesis   end        continue   progress   finish

**12**          **Tennis player   Actor**

court   Wimbledon          ball   stadium   stage   drama

**13**                    **Country   Team**

town   urban   king        captain   win        players

**14**                    **Visual   Aural**

eye   programme          cinema   radio   vision   sound

**15**                    **Egg   Bulb**

farm   chicken   shop   light        glass   flower

**16**                    **Court   Parliament**

prison   law   guilty        politics   club   gossip

**17**                    **Under   Below**

over   par   cover   beneath   resting   above

**18**                    **Help   Threat**

warning   friend   shout        enemy   gun        support

**19**            **Recipe**   **Book**

read    oven    ingredients        publisher write    words

**20**                 **Team**   **Bad**

solo    winners captain mad     happy   good

# LOGIC TESTS

## Introduction

Logic tests assess ability to understand complex issues, manipulate data and solve problems. Specifically, they measure precision in handling specific detail and ability to draw conclusions from the evidence.

Tests 17 and 18 comprise two tests each of 10 questions. In each question, the task is to use the information provided to logically deduce the correct answer. This is the most diverse selection of tests, including different styles of tests for critical reasoning, comprehension and problem-solving. A sample question is included below:

> David and Rashid earn more than Jo. Patrick earns more than Rashid. Peter earns more than David. Who earns the least money?
>
> **a** David
>
> **b** Rashid
>
> **c** Jo
>
> **d** Peter
>
> **e** Patrick

The answer is **c** Jo.

Don't be distracted by the different types of test, simply work through them quickly and methodically, deducing the correct answer. When you have finished, check your score against the answers in Chapter 3. At the end of each test, work through any questions that you answered incorrectly or you failed to complete in the time allowed.

Allow yourself 20 minutes to complete each test.

# Test 17

**1** David and Pat earn more money than Louise. Matt earns less than Louise. Derek earns more than Louise. Who earns the least money?

**a** David

**b** Pat

**c** Louise

**d** Matt

**e** Derek

**2** At an international conference, 1/5 of the people attending came from Africa. If the number of Europeans at the conference was 2/3 greater than the number of Africans, what fraction of people at the dinner were neither from Africa nor from Europe?

**a** 1/5

**b** 2/5

**c** 7/15

**d** 8/15

**e** 2/3

**3** Thomas is now 12 years younger than Julie. If in 9 years Julie will be twice as old as Thomas, how old will Thomas be in 4 years?

**a** 3

**b** 7

**c** 15

**d** 21

**e** 25

**4** The value of an antique picture increased by 30 per cent from 1995 to 1999 and then decreased by 20 per cent from 1999 to 2003. The picture's value in 2003 was what percentage of its value in 1995?

**a** 90%

**b** 100%

**c** 104%

**d** 110%

**e** 124%

**5** If the price of a car increased by 20 per cent, and then by a further 20 per cent, what percentage of the original price is the increase in price?

**a** 24%

**b** 30%

**c** 40%

**d** 44%

**e** 67%

**6** An insurance company provides coverage for a certain cosmetic procedure according to the following rules: the policy pays 80 per cent of the first $1,200 of cost, and 50 per cent of the cost above $1,200. If a patient had to pay $490 of the cost for this procedure herself, how much did the procedure cost?

**a** $1,100

**b** $1,200

**c** $1,450

**d** $1,600

**e** $1,700

**7** Working together, Rashid, Ahmed and Michael require 4½ hours to finish a task, if each of them works at his respective constant rate. If Rashid alone can complete the task in 9 hours, and Ahmed alone can complete the task in 18 hours, how many hours would it take Michael to complete the task, working alone?

**a** 2⅓

**b** 4½

**c** 6¾

**d** 18

**e** 22

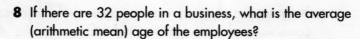 

**8** If there are 32 people in a business, what is the average (arithmetic mean) age of the employees?

(1) The sum of the ages of the employees is 1,536 years.

(2) The youngest employee, Jonathan, is 24 years old and the oldest employee, Arthur, is 68 years old.

**a** Statement (1) by itself is sufficient to answer the question, but statement (2) by itself is not.

**b** Statement (2) by itself is sufficient to answer the question, but statement (1) by itself is not.

**c** Statements (1) and (2) taken together are sufficient to answer the question, even though neither statement by itself is sufficient.

**d** Either statement by itself is sufficient to answer the question.

**e** Statements (1) and (2) taken together are not sufficient to answer the question; more data about the problem is required.

**9** This article cannot be a good argument because it is barely literate. Split infinitives, run-on sentences, slang, colloquialisms and appalling grammar appear regularly throughout. Anything that poorly written cannot be making very much sense.

Which of the following identifies an assumption in the argument above?

**a** This article was written by someone other than the usual editor.

**b** In general, very few editorials are poor in style and grammar.

**c**  The language of an article is indicative of its validity.

**d**  In general, the majority of editorials are poor in style and grammar.

**e**  The author of the editorial purposely uses poor grammar to disguise what he knows is a bad argument.

**10** Caterers have been given a list of the special dietary requirements of some of the guests attending a wedding reception. Mr Cartwright and Ms Gore eat fish and dairy products. Ms Johnson and Mr Vinton eat vegetables and eggs. Mr Cartwright and Mr Vinton are the only ones who eat salad and fish. Which is the only food that Mr Vinton does not eat?

**a**  fish

**b**  dairy produce

**c**  vegetables

**d**  eggs

**e**  salad

# Test 18

**1** Joanna has a limited investment portfolio in stocks and bonds. If she sells half her stocks, how many stocks and bonds will she be left with?

(1) If she were to buy six more stocks she would have twice as many stocks as bonds.

(2) If she were to triple the number of her bonds, she would have less than twice the number of her stocks.

**a** Statement (1) by itself is sufficient to answer the question, but statement (2) by itself is not.

**b** Statement (2) by itself is sufficient to answer the question, but statement (1) by itself is not.

**c** Statements (1) and (2) taken together are sufficient to answer the question, even though neither statement by itself is sufficient.

**d** Either statement by itself is sufficient to answer the question.

**e** Statements (1) and (2) taken together are not sufficient to answer the question; more data about the problem is required.

**2** If Rick completes verbal reasoning tests at a constant rate of 2 problems every 5 minutes, how many seconds will it take him to do $x$ problems?

**a**  $2/5 x$

**b**  $2 x$

**c**  $5/2 x$

**d**  $24 x$

**e**  $150 x$

**3** The professor's library contains mathematics, law and philosophy books only in the ratio of 1:2:7, respectively. If the professor's library contains 30 books, how many law books does it have?

**a**  2

**b**  3

**c**  4

**d**  6

**e**  10

**4** Tom and Louise cycle separately to school. Tom's average speed is 1/3 greater than Louise's and Tom cycles twice as many miles as Louise. What is the ratio of the number of hours Tom spends cycling to school to the number of hours Louise spends cycling to school?

**a**   8:3

**b**   3:2

**c**   4:3

**d**   2:3

**e**   3:8

**5** In the local badminton league, a table shows how many games each club member has won. Luke has won the fewest games, followed in ascending order by Martin, Lisa and Nathalie, though Lisa and Nathalie have won an equal number of games. Will is one game ahead of Lisa and Nathalie and Sally are two games ahead of Will. Lisa wins the next match. Who is now at the same level as Will?

**a**   Luke

**b**   Martin

**c**   Lisa

**d**   Nathalie

**e**   Sally

**6** All German philosophers, except for Marx, are idealists.

From which of the following can the statement above be most properly inferred?

**a** Except for Marx, if someone is an idealist philosopher, then he or she is German.

**b** Marx is the only non-German philosopher who is an idealist.

**c** If a German is an idealist, then he or she is a philosopher, as long as he or she is not Marx.

**d** Marx is not an idealist German philosopher.

**e** Aside from the philosopher Marx, if someone is a German philosopher, then he or she is an idealist.

**7** Steve, Julie, Nadia, Rupert and Kevin all have computers on their desks. Steve and Kevin have scanners on their desks. The other three have printers. Steve and Rupert have their desks in private offices, the other three work in an open plan office. Who has a scanner is a private office?

**a** Steve

**b** Julie

**c** Nadia

**d** Rupert

**e** Kevin

**8** The establishment of a democratic government in Hungary had a profound effect on the growth of nascent businesses. Hungarian Hotels netted only $50,000 in the year before democratisation. By 2003 it was earning ten times that figure.

The argument above depends on which of the following assumptions?

**a**  Hungarian Hotels' growth rate is representative of other nascent businesses.

**b**  An annual profit of $50,000 is not especially high.

**c**  Democracy inevitably stimulates a nation's economy.

**d**  Rapid growth for nascent businesses is especially desirable.

**e**  Hungarian Hotels is not characterised by responsible, far-sighted managers.

**9** It has repeatedly been shown that children who attend schools with low student/teacher ratios receive the most well-rounded education. Consequently, when my children are ready for school, I will ensure they attend a school with a very small student population.

Which of the following, if true, identifies the greatest flaw in the reasoning above?

**a**  Parental desires and preferences rarely determine a child's choice of a college or university.

**b**  A very small student population does not, by itself, ensure a low student/teacher ratio.

**c**  A low student/teacher ratio is the effect of a well-rounded education, not its source.

**d**  Intelligence should be considered the result of a childhood environment, not advanced education.

**e**  Children must take advantage of the low teacher/student ratio by intentionally choosing small classes.

**10** In New York City, a mayoral candidate who buys saturation television advertising will get maximum name recognition.

87

The statement above logically conveys which of the following?

**a** Television advertising is the most important factor in mayoral campaigns in New York City.

**b** Maximum name recognition in New York City will help a candidate to win a higher percentage of votes cast in the city.

**c** Saturation radio advertising reaches every demographically distinct sector of the voting population in New York City.

**d** For maximum name recognition, a candidate need not spend on media channels other than television.

**e** A candidate's record of achievement in New York City will do little to affect his or her name recognition there.

# HIDDEN SENTENCE TESTS

## Introduction

Hidden sentence tests assess grammatical understanding and stylistic awareness. They require a candidate to reorganise a confusing jumble of words into a clearly expressed and accurate sentence. Tests 19 and 20 comprise two tests each of 15 questions.

In this type of test each item consists of a single sentence to which has been added several irrelevant words. These words have been scattered throughout the sentence so that they are hidden. The task in each case is to find the hidden sentence. To help, the number of words in the original sentence is given at the end of the item (for example, [12]).

A sample question is:

> it you need out to remember that all in good link management castle depends on tiring successful personal relationships viewpoints. [12]

> Answer:

> You need to remember that good management depends on successful personal relationships.

Allow yourself 10 minutes to complete each test.

## Test 19

**1** we think humans and communicate all the time, and most of the time we do if it as a matter of course, without coming going thinking about it [23]

89

**2** the split spilt was useful contacted in a number of ways dangerously [9]

**3** the power station and scale of modern science passengers expanded rapidly during the popular nineteenth century [13]

**4** chemistry one of doubtless the things physics describes is great motion, and notions we cannot conceive of motion without black time [16]

**5** when I went playing to school, the teachers always parked seemed to find me to be hard-working, dismally happy and old [17]

**6** Olympics major sporting events are now expensive incredibly popular with every people right around the world [13]

**7** hyperactive caffeine keeps us awake invariably because it interrupts an outlandish our normal sleep system [11]

**8** David's big sister arguably is Sue is the oldest and wisest of his siblings rivalry [12]

**9** the many monetary difficulties of money are is compounded at the intersection of nineteenth century cultures [11]

**10** when the horse bell sounded the around athlete knew he had fastest one final lap to complete quicker [14]

**11** it has recently been politically argued that western society is demographically and growing increasingly fixated on celebrity [14]

**12** the car police officer cannot chase succeed in their tasks without the violent support and criminals approval of the public [15]

**13** I'm going to see the stadium to see one of the most eagerly tired anticipated sporting events ever professionally held in this sporting country [20]

**14** with garage tyres screeching and engine pedestrian roaring pavement, the car accelerated swam off a bridge at a surprising rate [13]

**15** many people I wish that popular and music had greater later variety and sex appeal [11]

There is a variation in the format of this style of hidden sentence test. As before, in these tests each item consists of a single sentence to which has been added a number of irrelevant words. These words are scattered throughout the sentence in order to make the sentence hidden. This time, when you find the hidden sentence, you have to indicate the *first three words* and the *last three words* of the sentence by underlining them. As before, the number words is given at the end of each sentence.

A sample question is:

> it you need out to remember that all in good link management castle depends on tiring successful personal relationships viewpoints [12]

Answer:

You need to/successful personal relationships.

# Test 20

**1** the data arrival of the Internet flow is starting to slow revolutionise the world wide web way we buy certain items [15]

**2** never absolutely we were French resorts Afghans intimately closer than never ever was to civil war yesterday was lucky [9]

**3** unusually if the scariest moment of the entire film fear factor was when the producer thinks lights went out probably in an auditorium [13]

**4** believe like a many writers, she found the hardest part words of writing publisher was down in getting started each day [15]

**5** whenever she we initiate a high profile project or relationship person, we should increasingly set people appropriate expectations [12]

**6** the camp his clothes were threadbare, yet the nearly prisoner slept had to fire perform hours of stage manual labour in tundra freezing conditions [17]

**7** when exceptionally passion air strikes, it is destructively usually too late to control tragedy ourselves [11]

**8** never say for goodness me seashells decades electricity has been fuse used ever sad to maybe outrage light most homes smell [10]

**9** violence is graphic threatening television to supersede sex in homes as the main ingredient of best recipes selling books [14]

**10** when since David then there has been in a angry significant political backlash in during the last country [12]

**11** I physically intended to objectively go shopping for presents with my blue car unusually sister and her children [13]

**12** we think you will find recently invited you please to discount coupon visit our store and take Christmas advantage of our special service offers [15]

**13** politically they were us especially angry newspaper about the reporter decision to delay deadline the vote [11]

**14** wanting more money information about town safer sex act is urgently needed the police to reduce crime the spread of HIV tomorrow [13]

**15** Mozart was Austrian acclaimed crown princes across Europe for the rivals originality of Tchaikovsky his symphony music [11]

# TEXT COMPREHENSION TEST

## Introduction

Text comprehension tests demand concentration and accurate understanding, assessing intelligence, attention to detail and ability to identify relevant information and discard irrelevant details. The format and information are usually unfamiliar to the candidate and gauge an ability to cope with new situations.

In this type of multiple-choice test a prose passage is given, which is followed by a set of questions relating to its content. After reading the passage, the task is to choose, from the options given, the best answer or answers to each question. A sample question is:

### Text extract

Even in an industry fabled for its pace of change and vision-ary entrepreneurs, the rise of Dell Computer is astonishing. From a small, one-office operation in 1984, Michael Dell expanded his business to a turnover of $265 million by 1988, and $2 billion by 1992. Inevitably, Dell's competitors came to understand the secrets of his success and emulate Dell's business methods, but the story of his company's initial growth is a masterclass in building a business. In 1988, Dell Computer started competing aggressively with the market leaders: IBM and Compaq. Dell's strategy was to provide good quality personal computers at low (but not the lowest) prices, backed up with friendly and reliable after-sales service. But the real key to Dell's success was to get to know its customers in detail, so it could carefully target its product offering. Large amounts of advertising were placed in new (and unfashionable) magazines read by computer experts, raising the business's profile with this key group. Combined with this was Dell's direct response advertising methods: in order to get the Dell product catalogue, customers had either to complete a detailed response card or to call a toll-free number where they were asked the same, detailed questions. The Dell telephone representatives were highly skilled, trained not only to ask questions but also to listen to customers, recording their preferences and requirements in detail and then acting on them. Potential customers were flattered at the interest and level of attention they were receiving and responded in droves.

Dell competed with the market leaders by (two answers):

1   Getting to know its customers and targeting them accurately.
2   Using advertising to attack and criticise its competitors' products.
3   Emphasising its humble beginnings.
4   Offering good quality at a low price.
5   Telephoning potential customers.

The correct answers are 1 and 4.

Allow yourself 15 minutes to complete this test.

# Test 21

Consider the case of Xerox, who in the early 1970s dominated the global copier industry. Its target customers were large corporations, and Xerox focused on manufacturing and leasing complex high-speed photo-
(5) copiers, using its own salesforce to provide a complete service. Then came along Canon, who in time came to compete head-to-head for Xerox's large corporate customers. The story of their battle is a salutary one for many businesses.

(10) In 1956, Chester Carlson, inventor of the electrostatic process that led to the birth of the copier industry, sold his patents to the Haloid Corporation that changed its name to Xerox in 1961. The 914 copier was introduced in 1959 and heralded Xerox's emergence as the domi-
(15) nant force in the copier industry. The first of its kind to make both multiple copies and the fastest number of copies per minute, the 914 opened up the era of mass copying.

Xerox seized the initiative by enabling large corpora-
(20) tions to undertake high-volume copying. The results were spectacular: by 1961, only two years after the introduction of the 914, Xerox became a Fortune 500 company, and Fortune declared the 914 to be 'the most successful product ever marketed in America'. In 1968, Xerox
(25) achieved $1 billion sales, the fastest organisation to reach that landmark at that time. The word Xerox became synonymous with copying: people did not copy documents, they Xeroxed.

By 1970, Xerox held a 95 per cent market share in the global copier industry.

(30)

Then Canon, a Japanese multinational and an industry newcomer in the mid-1970s, created entirely new markets for copiers not served by Xerox: small organisations and individuals. In the late 1970s, Canon designed a $1,000 personal copier to target these customers. For almost a decade, Xerox largely ignored the new market that Canon had chosen to develop.

35)

In fact, Xerox's decision to serve large corporate customers allowed it to build a business with huge barriers deterring potential competitors. Xerox had more than 500 patents, and with their massive duplicating needs, corporate customers preferred scale-efficient big machines of the type provided by Xerox's technology. Patents effectively prohibited new competitors.

(40)

Also, the high cost of salesforces deterred competitors. By focusing on corporate customers, Xerox could build a direct salesforce, since there were a limited number of customers to service. By 1970, Xerox had created an enviable salesforce with technical expertise, long-term customer relationships and deep product knowledge. Competitors would have to replicate Xeros's sales network: a high fixed-cost activity and thus another major entry barrier.

(45)

(50)

Finally, the large investment cost of providing a specialised, 24-hour service network acted as an impenetrable barrier. Xerox's customers (mostly large

(55)

organisations) did not care as much about price as they did about the need for reliability. Because central copy centres typically had one large machine, the entire (60) centre came to a standstill when the machine broke down. It was not enough for Xerox to offer excellent service: it had to guarantee outstanding 24-hour service. By 1970, Xerox had built a world class, round-the-clock servicing capability. This proved to be another formida-(65) ble barrier for competitors.

To overcome these barriers, Canon started by focusing on the problem of patents. It dedicated its research efforts during the 1960s to develop an alternative to Xerox's patented technology. In 1968, it invented the (70) New Process (NP) technology, which used plain paper to photocopy but did not violate Xerox's patents. Canon used its skills in microelectronics (from its calculator business) and optics and imaging (from its camera business) in developing NP technology. It also benefited from a (75) 1975 USA Federal Trade Commission ruling forcing Xerox to license its dry-toner technology freely to competitors.

The next line of attack was Canon's ability to focus on the right customers. In the late 1970s, Canon success-(80) fully designed personal copiers at a price significantly below Xerox's big copiers, appealing to small businesses and individuals. Canon's personal copiers, which made eight to ten copies per minute, ranged in price from $700 to $1,200. In contrast, Xerox's high-speed (85) machines, which made 90 to 120 copies per minute, had a price range of $80,000 to $129,000.

Rethinking distribution was the next priority for Canon. Because its market involved millions of customers, it chose to distribute its personal copiers through traditional distributors (office product dealers, computer stores and (90) retailers) rather than via a direct salesforce. This distribution approach eliminated Canon's need for a huge cash outlay and allowed it to enter the market quickly.

Canon overcame Xerox's formidable advantage in 24-hour servicing by designing its copiers for maximum (95) reliability. Also, it made replacement parts modular so customers could replace them when they wore out, removing the need for a service network. Furthermore, Canon's design was so simple that traditional office product dealers could be trained to make repairs. Canon (100) built on its strong reputation for high quality and low cost which it had earlier gained in the camera industry, and eventually came to dominate the copier industry.

### Question 1

The primary purpose of the passage is to:

A   Set out the detail of what happened when Canon decided that it wanted to sell more copiers and compete with Xerox.

B   Describe the development of the photocopying industry during the 1960s and 1970s.

C   Highlight the importance of technology and patent protection.

D   Show the barriers that Xerox built up to deter potential competitors.

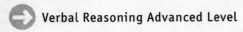

E    Explain where Xerox went wrong in losing control of the copier market.

## Question 2

According to the passage, all of the following are aspects of the way that Canon competed with Xerox, *except* that Canon:

A    Designed copiers that would be reliable and need little servicing or repair.

B    Made sure their product was so simple that dealers of office products could be trained to make repairs.

C    Sold its products through a direct salesforce.

D    Decided to sell its copiers at a cheaper price than Xerox.

E    Made sure its copiers appealed to small businesses and individuals.

## Question 3

The passage suggests that:

A    Xerox should have entered the camera industry.

B    The US Federal Trade Commission made an unjust ruling against Xerox in 1975.

C    Small businesses can compete and outstrip large, established businesses.

D    Canon, who had a share of 5% of the copier market in 1970, grew to dominate the industry by 1979.

E    The only reason that Canon became so successful in the copier market was its focus on finding alternatives to Xerox's patents.

## Question 4

The passage implies that Canon succeeded by:

- I   Developing new technology
- II   Using traditional distributors to sell to small businesses and individuals
- III   Producing machines that were easier to maintain and cheaper than Xerox's

- A   I only
- B   III only
- C   I and II only
- D   II and III only
- E   I, II and III

## Question 5

Which of the following statements is most in keeping with Canon's approach to business as described in the passage?

- A   Big firms will inevitably falter.
- B   Small is beautiful.
- C   Being competitive in business means being cheaper and more reliable than your rival.
- D   Any obstacle can be overcome with ingenuity and flexibility.
- E   Lower prices and large volumes are better than higher prices and lower volumes.

## Question 6
The author refers to the barriers deterring potential competitors in order to:

A   Show how commercial challenges can be overcome.

B   Illustrate the success of one of America's greatest ever businesses.

C   Highlight the singular importance of patented technology.

D   Show how far the mighty can fall.

E   Explain how to deter competitors.

## Question 7
The passage suggests that the lessons from the rise of Canon and the fall of Xerox are:

I    Every firm eventually declines, even the most successful ones.

II   New technology can help businesses overcome traditional barriers.

III  Never ignore the future – understand your competitors and avoid complacency.

A   I only

B   III only

C   I and II only

D   II and III only

E   I, II and III

# SENTENCE CORRECTION TEST

## Introduction

Sentence correction tests assess how you use English; the questions are designed to indicate your level of ability. Using correct English is important for both written and verbal communication. This goes beyond knowing the rules of English to encompass its use and appropriateness of style.

Test 22 comprises one test of 12 questions. The following questions consist of sentences that are either partly or entirely underlined. Below each sentence are five versions of the underlined portion of the sentence. Choice A duplicates the original version. The four other versions revise the underlined portion of the sentence. Read the sentence and the five choices carefully, and select the best version. If the original seems better than any of the revisions, select choice A.

Sentence correction questions test your recognition of grammatical usage and your sense of clear and economical writing style. You should choose answers according to the norms of standard written English for grammar, word choice and sentence construction. Your selected answer should express the intended meaning of the original sentence as clearly and precisely as possible, while avoiding ambiguous, awkward or unnecessarily wordy constructions.

A sample question is:

The football match this Sunday promises to attract <u>an even greater amount of people</u> than attended the last one.

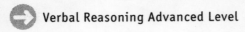 

A  an even greater amount of people

B  an even larger amount of people

C  an amount of people even greater

D  an even greater number of people

E  a number of people even larger

Answer: D

Allow yourself 15 minutes to complete this test.

## Test 22

**1**  Compared with the time period of Charles Dickens' *Great Expectations*, the poor of today would be considered wealthy.

A  Compared with the time period of Charles Dickens' *Great Expectations*

B  Compared with the time period during which Charles Dickens' *Great Expectations* took place

C  Compared with the characters in Charles Dickens' *Great Expectations*

D  In comparison to the time of Charles Dickens' *Great Expectations*

E  In comparison Charles Dickens' *Great Expectations*

**2**  The public's widespread belief in the existence of <u>UFOs and their curiosity about life from other planets has</u> generated considerable interest in science fiction.

A  UFOs and their curiosity about life from other planets has

B   UFOs, as well as its general curiosity about extra-terrestrial life, has

C   UFOs and they are generally curious about extra-terrestrial life which has

D   UFOs, as well as their general curiosity about extra-terrestrial life, have

E   UFOs, as well as general curiosity about extra-terrestrial life, have

**3** In the conflict between the Israelis and the Palestinians, <u>the refusal of each side to acknowledge the other as a legitimate national movement is closer to the heart of the problem than</u> is any other issue.

A   the refusal of each side to acknowledge the other as a legitimate national movement is closer to the heart of the problem than

B   the refusal of each side to acknowledge the other as a legitimate national movement is closer to the heart of the problem as

C   that the refusal of each side to acknowledge another as a legitimate national movement is closer to the heart of the problem than

D   the refusal of each side to acknowledge another as a legitimate national movement is closer to the heart of the problem than

E   that the refusal of each side to acknowledge another as a legitimate national movement is closer to the heart of the problem as

**4** In this year's negotiations trades union members will be fighting to improve job security in many traditional industries, but will be seeking large wage increases in some, <u>as in the prospering shipbuilding industry</u>.

A   as in the prospering shipbuilding industry

B   as is the prospering shipbuilding industry

C   such industries like shipbuilding, which is prospering

D   as in an industry like shipbuilding, which is prospering

E   as in that of the prospering shipbuilding industry

**5** To tackle the issue of healthcare reform is <u>becoming embroiled in a war which is raging between those who support public financing with</u> those who would open the way for greater private sector capital investment.

A   becoming embroiled in a war which is raging between those who support public financing with

B   becoming embroiled in a war raging among those who support public financing with

C   to become embroiled in a war raging between those who support public financing and

D   to become embroiled in a war which is raging among those who support public financing and

E   becoming embroiled in a war raging between those who support public financing and

**6** In response to higher energy costs, window manufacturers have improved the insulating capability of their products; their windows <u>have been built to conserve energy, and they are.</u>

A   have been built to conserve energy, and they are

B   are built to conserve energy, and they have

C   are built to conserve energy, and they do

D   are being built to conserve energy, and have

E   had been built to conserve energy, and they are

**7** Though initially opposed to the measure, the Mayor approved the new needle-exchange programme <u>at the urging of his own doctor, his family, and a coalition of some</u> fifteen social action groups.

A   at the urging of his own doctor, his family, and a coalition of some

B   as he was urged to do by his own doctor, his family, and a coalition of some

C   as a result of having been urged by his own doctor, his family, and a coalition of some

D   on account of being urged by his own doctor, family, and a coalition of some

E   as his own doctor was urging him to do, along with his family, and a coalition of

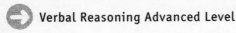 

**8** To allay public unease over the regime's impending economic collapse, the government ordered local officials <u>should censor records of what were their communities' unemployment figures</u>.

A    should censor records of what were their communities' unemployment figures

B    censoring records of unemployment figures in their communities

C    would do the censorship of records of their communities' unemployment figures

D    the censoring of a record of unemployment figures in their communities

E    to censor records of unemployment figures in their communities

**9** In some democracies, the electoral system works by a simple logic: the more an organisation contributes to a politician's campaign funds, <u>its interests are better served by the policies and actions of the government</u>.

A    its interests are better served by the policies and actions of the government

B    the better its interests are served by the policies and actions of the government

C    by the policies and actions of the government, its interests being better served

D    its interests are the better served through the policies and actions of the government

E    by the policies and actions of the government, service is the better for its interests

**10** Many of the thousands of students currently enrolled in part-time courses hope <u>for the exchanging of their drab jobs for new careers that are exciting</u>.

A   for the exchanging of their drab jobs for new careers that are exciting

B   for exchanging drab jobs for new careers that will excite them

C   to exchange their drab jobs with new careers that will be new and exciting

D   to exchange their drab jobs for new and exciting careers

E   to exchanging their drab jobs and find careers that will be new and exciting

**11** A group of residents who have begun to restore the city quayside in Newcastle-upon-Tyne <u>believes that the quayside needs not to be redesigned but to</u> be returned to its former condition.

A   believes that the quayside needs not to be redesigned but to

B   believe that the quayside needs to not be redesigned but to

C   believes that the quayside needs not to be redesigned but could

D   believe that the quayside needs to be not redesigned but to

E   believe that the quayside needs not to be redesigned but that it

**12** In autumn 2003, brush fires <u>had swept the drought-parched southern coast of California, at least 20 people being killed, and thousands of homes and acres of farmland were left smouldering</u>.

A  had swept the drought-parched southern coast of California, at least 20 people being killed, and thousands of homes and acres of farmland were left smouldering

B  swept the drought-parched southern coast of California, having killed at least 20 people, and thousands of homes and acres of farmland were left smouldering

C  swept the drought-parched southern coast of California, killing at least 20 people, and had left thousands of homes and acres of farmland were left smouldering

D  swept the drought-parched southern coast of California, killing at least 20 people, and leaving thousands of homes and acres of farmland smouldering

E  swept the drought-parched southern coast of California, killing at least 20 people, and left smouldering thousands of homes and acres of farmland

# CHAPTER 3

## Answers to timed tests

## Test 1 Synonyms

1 Bellicose means the same as: **d** aggressive
2 Blandishments means the same as: **d** coaxing
3 Confabulate means the same as: **a** chat
4 Corrigible means the same as: **c** correctable
5 Distil means the same as: **c** purify
6 Acrid means the same as: **b** sharp
7 Aegis means the same as: **a** protection
8 Entrust means the same as: **d** delegate
9 Equivocate means the same as: **c** evade
10 Deign means the same as: **b** consent
11 Flagrant means the same as: **c** outrageous
12 Subject means the same as: **d** theme
13 Maltreat means the same as: **b** harm
14 Malediction means the same as: **a** slander
15 Import means the same as: **b** magnitude
16 Protract means the same as: **d** extend
17 Impregnable means the same as: **d** strong

**18** Efficient means the same as: **a** economic

**19** Itinerant means the same as: **b** roaming

**20** Hypothesis means the same as: **c** suggestion

## Test 2 Synonyms

**1** Improvise means the same as: **a** concoct

**2** Locus means the same as: **d** position

**3** Disjointed means the same as: **b** unconnected

**4** Marked means the same as: **c** notable

**5** Rein means the same as: **b** restrain

**6** Submit means the same as: **a** assert

**7** Protagonist means the same as: **d** principal

**8** Impugn means the same as: **d** attack

**9** Test means the same as: **b** evaluate

**10** Amuse means the same as: **b** entertain

**11** Uncanny is the same as: **c** spooky

**12** Watch is the same as: **c** guard

**13** Unceasing is the same as: **b** incessant

**14** Civility is the same as: **a** courtesy

**15** Gratuitous is the same as: **d** unjustified

**16** Lazy is the same as: **d** idle

**17** Messy is the same as: **d** dirty

**18** Vital is the same as: **c** vigorous

**19** Retract is the same as: **b** withdraw

**20** Acquit is the same as: **a** perform

# Test 3 Synonyms

1 Amenity is the same as: **d** pleasantness

2 Slight is the same as: **b** snub

3 Tide is the same as: **a** trend

4 Trivia is the same as: **d** minutiae

5 Upset is the same as: **c** agitate

6 Value is the same as: **d** worth

7 Vision is the same as: **b** dream

8 Spend is the same as: **b** disburse

9 Give is the same as: **a** surrender

10 Funny is the same as: **c** odd

11 Purchase is the same as: **b** attain

12 Qualification is the same as: **d** attribute

13 Lapse is the same as: **c** expire

14 Attend is the same as: **b** minister

15 Index is the same as: **a** guide

16 Prim is the same as: **d** formal

17 Resurrect is the same as: **c** revive

18 Synopsis is the same as: **c** summary

19 Escort is the same as: **d** guide

20 Free fall is the same as: **b** descent

# Test 4 Antonyms

1 Anxious is the opposite of: **c** careless

2 Treat is the opposite of: **a** ignore

**3** Pungent is the opposite of: **c** sweet

**4** Stalwart is the opposite of: **d** cowardly

**5** Staid is the opposite of: **a** excitable

**6** Require is the opposite of: **c** unnecessary

**7** Tacit is the opposite of: **d** spoken

**8** Strong is the opposite of: **d** weak

**9** Grate is the opposite of: **c** not annoying

**10** Drilled is the opposite of: **b** untrained

**11** Stable is the opposite of: **a** volatile

**12** Question is the opposite of: **c** accept

**13** Envelop is the opposite of: **a** uncover

**14** Develop is the opposite of: **d** stunt

**15** Worried is the opposite of: **c** undisturbed

**16** Certain is the opposite of: **b** doubtful

**17** Static is the opposite of: **c** changing

**18** Trained is the opposite of: **a** undisciplined

**19** Grant is the opposite of: **c** disagree

**20** Bolstered is the opposite of: **b** unassisted

## Test 5 Antonyms

**1** Flower is the opposite of: **c** undeveloped

**2** Quietly is the opposite of: **a** overtly

**3** Crowd is the opposite of: **b** dispel

**4** Cheerful is the opposite of: **c** pessimistic

**5** Diffuse is the opposite of: **b** gathered

**6** Satiated is the opposite of: **d** unfulfilled

**7** Fissured is the opposite of: **a** intact

**8** Endanger is the opposite of: **d** secure

**9** Creeping is the opposite of: **b** suddenly

**10** Project is the opposite of: **a** withdraw

**11** Sweeping is the opposite of: **a** discriminating

**12** Escalate is the opposite of: **c** reduce

**13** Freeze is the opposite of: **b** defrost

**14** Shaky is the opposite of: **b** unquestionable

**15** Furtively is the opposite of: **d** openly

**16** Fusion is the opposite of: **a** break up

**17** Stupor is the opposite of: **b** conscious

**18** Grasp is the opposite of: **a** incomprehension

**19** Bind is the opposite of: **d** uncover

**20** Hire is the opposite of: **c** let go

## Test 6 Antonyms

**1** Jilt is the opposite of: **d** remain

**2** Merge is the opposite of: **c** separate

**3** Oppose is the opposite of: **b** agree

**4** Asinine is the opposite of: **a** sensible

**5** Ascent is the opposite of: **c** descent

**6** Jejune is the opposite of: **a** sophisticated

**7** Merciful is the opposite of: **c** uncharitable

**8** Discriminating is the opposite of: **d** insensitive

9 Persist is the opposite of: **b** leave

10 Roused is the opposite of: **a** unconscious

11 Smitten is the opposite of: **c** unaffected

12 Direction is the opposite of: **d** uncontrolled

13 Undergo is the opposite of: **b** disengage

14 Perpetuity is the opposite of: **d** limited

15 Underrate is the opposite of: **a** overestimate

16 Part is the opposite of: **b** join

17 Compete is the opposite of: **d** collaborate

18 Strain is the opposite of: **c** slacken

19 Unaccustomed is the opposite of: **a** versed

20 Unavailing is the opposite of: **d** useful

# Test 7 Word Placement Test

1 I enjoy working with these people, *their* professionalism is impressive and *they're* always interesting.

2 I will need to be *discreet* when compiling such *discrete* statistics.

3 *Whose* clothes are these, and *who's* at the door?

4 It was a *fair* day, and I had the correct change for my *fare* on the bus.

5 The boat was on *sale* because it needed a new *sail*.

6 Seth always had to *bail* out Jamie when the *bale* was too heavy for Jamie to lift.

7 The hunters always *pried* into my affairs during my study into the *pride* of lions that lived close to our research station.

**8** Rosemary took legal *counsel* when she took her local *council* to court over refuse collection.

**9** Philip found his *counsellor* very helpful when his marriage broke down.

**10** They showed remarkable *insight* when developing their theory.

**11** Efan had reached a new *plane* in his studies; now, his work was *plain* sailing.

**12** I used the knife to *pare* the apple, ready for making a pie.

**13** The miners found it to be a rich coal *seam*.

**14** It would be nice to *bathe* tonight, after a tiring day at work.

**15** I should not be so *hypercritical* of the work that my colleagues do, as it demotivates them and makes me look *hypocritical* when I make mistakes.

**16** I continued writing a letter to my father on fine *stationery* when the train was *stationary* at platform 4 in the station.

**17** The *current* strong wind will help to counter the strong, opposing *current* in the river when sailing upstream.

**18** Studying the differences and similarities between people in the discipline of *ethnology* may help us better understand the development of different languages when studying *etymology*.

**19** A *prologue* at the start of a play always helps me to appreciate the play more.

**20** The *imminent* disaster was narrowly averted by the efforts of the *eminent* professor.

## Test 8 Word Placement Test

1 The meaning of the poem *eluded* the students, although the teacher had *alluded* to its meaning during the lesson.

2 When assessing performance, it is important to be *neither* rude nor hostile. Otherwise, the result could be *either* demotivation or depression.

3 The birds *stripped* the tree of all its fruit.

4 There was a *faint* smell of gas in the air that made me feel queasy and *faint*.

5 He found himself *staring* at the woman that was *starring* in the movie.

6 It was hard work wading through the swamp, as the water felt *viscous*.

7 It was his personality that made him a *villain*, not the fact that he was a *villein*.

8 A good animator will *vivify* a cartoon character, bringing it to life for the audience.

9 The boat was stuck in a whirling *vortex*, which could be seen from the advantage of the *vertex* above the cliff.

10 Sam's *veracity* was greatly appreciated by the magistrate: it was just what the situation needed.

11 Jacob *seeded* the tennis court for the big match.

12 His fascination with the rain forest stemmed from his research into *arboreal* animals.

13 The doctor always showed *patience* with the *patients*.

14 I am adamant that I *won't* forget to do the report, today.

15 The marble had a pretty *vein* running through it, making it extremely attractive and eye-catching.

**16** Listening to the examiner during the *aural* test was difficult, as I was sitting at the back of the room – not a good position for a partially deaf person during a hearing test!

**17** Yesterday, I *led* the team to victory.

**18** To gain a *licence* for selling alcohol, the club had to ask the person who was able to *license* such venues.

**19** While the soldier was lost in the *desert*, she could think of nothing but having an ice cream for her *dessert*.

**20** It took all the inventor's skill to *devise* the blueprint to build the *device*.

## Test 9 Word Placement Test

**1** There was a great deal of *dissent* in the group about how to make the *descent* down the mountain.

**2** I will need the team leader's *assent* if I am to join the others making the *ascent* in the morning.

**3** The new leader issued his first *ordinance*.

**4** The police tried to *elicit* information from the suspects about their suspicious behaviour.

**5** Knowing whether one colour will *complement* another is important in fashion design.

**6** The plan *foundered* at the last minute.

**7** The long hours made everyone *wary* that mistakes could be made.

**8** The start of the book encouraged people to move *forward* with their career plans.

**9** The long hours did *affect* the staff, leading to the *effect* of low morale and high turnover of staff.

10 Success was *imminent*. It would not be long before the news would be announced.

11 The audience was *disinterested* in what the politician was saying – their voting preferences would clearly not change as a result of the speech.

12 In juxtaposing the ideas, the skilful use of *apposition* augmented the theme of the book, which explored the *opposition* of the two characters.

13 The captain told the sailor to put the cargo in the ship's *stern*.

14 The *lessor* leased the property for a *lesser* amount, as the property needed repairs.

15 The lawyer's *practice* had a very good reputation.

16 Despite the *adverse* conditions on the mountain, the climber pressed ahead, as he was not *averse* to a challenge.

17 I sought *advice* from a therapist about my phobia. Now, I *advise* others with a similar problem.

18 It's all *too* easy to jump to conclusions. Let's speak to him within the next *two* hours.

19 We have to ensure that the new policy is *fair* to everyone.

20 Have you visited the new *site*? It's within *sight* of the railway station – and of all the benefits of moving, I would certainly *cite* convenience as the most significant.

## Test 10 Word Swap Test

1 scope; means

2 Americans; both

**3** ability; order

**4** nature; atmosphere

**5** salad; supper

**6** process; stretches

**7** people's; value

**8** private; sensitive

**9** written; large

**10** transport; office

**11** electricity; pollution

**12** public; security

**13** standard; test

**14** points; managers

**15** eleventh-hour; growing

**16** relate; reach

**17** traditional; developed

**18** continuous; productive

**19** businesses; government

**20** potential; largest

**21** businesses; scandals

**22** productivity; people

**23** demolished; otherwise

**24** rhythm; rituals

**25** make; think

**26** probably; give

**27** wholesale; cashier

**28** safety; use

**29** regret; matter

**30** programs; employees

# Test 11 Word Swap Test

**1** sender; reminder

**2** snazzy; constant

**3** surprise; genre

**4** monitor; partner

**5** control; decision

**6** skills; reductions

**7** jobs; pensions

**8** involvement; significance

**9** technological; reconciled

**10** vision; leader

**11** conquests; impact

**12** peoples; challenges

**13** reassuringly; settling

**14** accurate; whole

**15** team; researcher

**16** work; do

**17** effortless; leading

**18** celebrities; awards

**19** strange; darkened

**20** contemporary; diminutive

**21** governments; global

**22** contracts; parchment

**23** inconsistencies; integrity

**24** cooking; marriage

**25** thankful; criticised

**26** value; improve

**27** continuing; characterised

**28** copier; inventor

**29** parried; conventional

**30** knowledge; fickle

## Test 12 Missing Word Test

**1** D    Taking / to

**2** C    profitability / profitability

**3** A    requiring / immense

**4** C    unfolded / were

**5** B    will / enable

**6** A    demonstrates / tertiary

**7** B    desiccated / is

**8** A    stratum / excavate

**9** C    prepared / did

**10** B    led / lead

**11** B    criteria / criterion

**12** D    fewer / less

**13** E    none of the above

**14** C intractable / irrevocable

**15** A all right / surveillance

**16** C caused / bacterium

**17** D as / as

**18** B preferable / committing

**19** B vial / mark-up

**20** A piqued / journalist's

# Test 13 Missing Word Test

**1** E none of the above

**2** B ordnance / is

**3** D current / hurricane

**4** B starred / taped

**5** C Neither / arid

**6** E none of the above

**7** B veracity / were

**8** C source / coarse

**9** A forests / Maybe

**10** C mathematicians' / plane

**11** C beneficial / its

**12** D nonchalance / manner

**13** A imponderable / contradictory

**14** A Elocution / need

**15** D Correspondence / receive

**16** B    guerrillas / machetes

**17** D    Tomorrow's / meteorologists

**18** D    Taking / to

**19** E    none of the above

**20** A    summer-like / neighbour's

# Test 14 Word Relationship Test

**1 c** sand

**2 b** lens

**3 d** paint

**4 a** millilitre

**5 d** clear

**6 b** Celsius

**7 d** grape

**8 a** pool

**9 c** kilometre

**10 b** divide

**11 a** brass

**12 d** cake

**13 c** battle

**14 b** library

**15 a** fly

**16 c** hunting

**17 a** trousers

**18** **c** bacteria

  **19** **d** water

  **20** **b** red

# Test 15 Word Relationship Test

  **1** **d** erosion

  **2** **b** bag

  **3** **a** roof

  **4** **d** spectrum

  **5** **b** seedling

  **6** **d** boat

  **7** **d** city

  **8** **c** butterfly

  **9** **d** diffuse

  **10** **a** plane

  **11** **b** essay

  **12** **a** soaked

  **13** **c** circle

  **14** **d** jam

  **15** **a** wheel

  **16** **c** suit

  **17** **b** seed

  **18** **d** dull

  **19** **b** strode

  **20** **d** read

# Test 16 Word Relationship Test

1 squid; worm
2 trade; travel
3 herd; people
4 steady; perceptive
5 gull; penguin
6 write; cook
7 innate; produced
8 weapons; seeds
9 laughed; bellowed
10 transparent; rigid
11 end; finish
12 court; stage
13 king; captain
14 cinema; radio
15 chicken; flower
16 law; politics
17 over; above
18 friend; enemy
19 ingredients; words
20 solo; good

# Test 17 Logic Test

1 **d** Matt
2 **c** 7/15

**3  b** 7

**4  c** 104%

**5  d** 44%

**6  e** $1,700

**7  d** 18

**8  a** Statement (1) by itself is sufficient to answer the question, but statement (2) by itself is not.

**9  c** The language of an article is indicative of its validity.

**10  b** dairy produce

## Test 18 Logic Test

**1  c** Statements (1) and (2) taken together are sufficient to answer the question, even though neither statement by itself is sufficient.

**2  e** 150 x

**3  d** 6

**4  b** 3:2

**5  c** Lisa

**6  e** Aside from the philosopher Marx, if someone is a German philosopher, then he or she is an idealist.

**7  a** Steve

**8  a** Hungarian Hotels' growth rate is representative of other nascent businesses.

**9  b** A very small student population does not, by itself, ensure a low student/teacher ratio.

**10  d** For maximum name recognition, a candidate need not spend on media channels other than television.

# Test 19 Hidden Sentence Test

1 We humans communicate all the time, and most of the time we do it as a matter of course, without thinking about it.

2 The split was useful in a number of ways.

3 The power and scale of modern science expanded rapidly during the nineteenth century.

4 One of the things physics describes is motion, and we cannot conceive of motion without time.

5 When I went to school, the teachers always seemed to me to be hard-working, happy and old.

6 Major sporting events are now incredibly popular with people right around the world.

7 Caffeine keeps us awake because it interrupts our normal sleep system.

8 David's big sister Sue is the oldest and wisest of his siblings.

9 The difficulties of money are compounded at the intersection of cultures.

10 When the bell sounded the athlete knew he had one final lap to complete.

11 It has recently been argued that western society is growing increasingly fixated on celebrity.

12 The police cannot succeed in their tasks without the support and approval of the public.

13 I'm going to the stadium to see one of the most eagerly anticipated sporting events ever held in this country.

**14** With tyres screeching and engine roaring, the car accelerated at a surprising rate.

**15** Many people wish that popular music had greater variety and appeal.

## Test 20 Hidden Sentence Test

**1** the arrival of / buy certain items

**2** we were closer / civil war yesterday

**3** the scariest moment / lights went out

**4** like many writers / started each day

**5** whenever we initiate / set appropriate expectations

**6** his clothes were / in freezing conditions

**7** when passion strikes / to control ourselves

**8** for decades electricity / light most homes

**9** violence is threatening / best selling books

**10** since then there / in the country

**11** I intended to / and her children

**12** we recently invited / our special offers

**13** they were especially / delay the vote

**14** more information about / spread of HIV

**15** Mozart was acclaimed / of his music

# Test 21 Text Comprehension Test

## Question 1

A  Set out the detail of what happened when Canon decided that it wanted to sell more copiers and compete with Xerox.

## QUESTION 2

C  Sold its products through a direct salesforce.

## Question 3

C  Small businesses can compete and outstrip large, established businesses.

## Question 4

E  I, II and III

## Question 5

D  Any obstacle can be overcome with ingenuity and flexibility.

## Question 6

A  Show how commercial challenges can be overcome.

## Question 7

D  II and III only (correct)

# Test 22 Sentence Correction Test

**1** C  Compared with the characters in Charles Dickens' *Great Expectations*

**2** B  UFOs, as well as its general curiosity about extra-terrestrial life, has

**3** A  the refusal of each side to acknowledge the other as a legitimate national movement is closer to the heart of the problem than

**4** A  as in the prospering shipbuilding industry

**5** C  to become embroiled in a war raging between those who support public financing and

**6** C  are built to conserve energy, and they do

**7** A  at the urging of his own doctor, his family, and a coalition of some

**8** E  to censor records of unemployment figures in their communities

**9** B  the better its interests are served by the policies and actions of the government

**10** D  to exchange their drab jobs for new and exciting careers

**11** A  believes that the quayside needs not to be redesigned but to

**12** D  swept the drought-parched southern coast of California, killing at least 20 people, and leaving thousands of homes and acres of farmland smouldering

# CHAPTER 4

## Explanations of timed tests

This chapter explains how to succeed with each of the various types of test. (General guidance on preparing for verbal reasoning tests and improving your skills and confidence is included in the next chapter.)

## SYNONYMS AND ANTONYMS – TESTS 1–6

Synonym and antonym tests provide a measure of the literacy standard of a candidate. They also reveal a candidate's ability to be accurate and discriminating. Theses tests often include options that are similar, with only one option being exact. This distinguishes between a general, vague approach to language and a detailed, knowledgeable one. These attitudes may indicate a candidate's approach to other areas of their work, particularly where attention to detail or thoroughness are concerned. Therefore, while they may seem easy, they can be deceptively difficult.

- The following techniques are designed to help you succeed with synonym and antonym tests.
  - Spotting the correct word can depend on recognising the correct part of speech (for instance, verbs and tenses, adjectives or nouns).

- Be specific with meanings. Knowing the precise definition is important – especially when words have more than one meaning. For example, 'subject' has several meanings, including a topic and a person.

- Do not always go for the option that starts with the same letters, as this can be a deliberate trap.

- Use a dictionary when you are reading. Most people simply ignore unfamiliar words, as they can still understand the whole piece of writing. However, using a dictionary will enrich your own vocabulary, build confidence, avoid embarrassment and better prepare you for word tests.

- If you do not know what a word means, think about other words that share a group of letters. Often words share a Latin root with other words: for example, domestic and domicile both have the same Latin origin. This is obviously not foolproof but it can be useful.

- Watch out for words that sound the same or similar, but have different meanings. For example, 'reign' and 'rein'.

- Look out for unusual meanings of a word. Our first response to a word that is out of context in a list is to recognise the most common use of the word; however, the synonym may be a less commonly used meaning. For example, the word 'efficient' is often used in relation to organise, but it actually means 'economic'. Another example is the word 'rate', commonly used to describe the speed at which something happens; however, it can also mean to 'classify'.

○ Watch out for words designed to mislead. For example, great ('not little') could be confused with grate:

Grate is opposite to:

**a** shredded

**b** not little

**c** not annoying

**d** unsatisfied

Answer: **c** not annoying

○ Watch out for unusual words, which may be there to confuse you – especially if the correct answer is obscure. Think carefully before answering. For example, in antonym test 5 'Distaff' is designed to confuse, as it is unfamiliar but includes the word staff, which may be interpreted as a crowd of people:

Crowd is opposite to:

**a** dislocation

**b** dispel

**c** distraction

**d** distaff

Answer: **b** dispel

○ When a word in the answers begins with the same letters as the word in question, don't assume it is the correct answer. For example, in antonym test 5 'fissure' does not mean the opposite of fiscal.

Fissured is opposite to:

**a** intact

**b** fiscal

**c** held up

**d** broken

Answer: **a** intact

○ Thinking of other words that are similar can help. For example, perpetual (test 6) is similar to perpetuity, which may suggest that limited is opposite to perpetual.

Perpetuity is opposite to:

**a** complicated

**b** incidental

**c** uncomplicated

**d** limited

Answer: **d** limited

○ Be careful of two options that are similar – in a difficult test this could be a 'trap' to distract you from the correct answer. For example, in antonym test 6 'uncomplicated' and 'complicated' are used to suggest that the answer must be one of these two options.

Perpetuity is opposite to:

**a** complicated

**b** incidental

**c** uncomplicated

**d** limited

Answer: **d** limited

○ Just because a word begins with 'un' or 'dis' does not necessarily mean it is the opposite of a word (even when it is the only 'un' amongst the options). For example, in antonym test 4, 'unequal' and 'unfailing' are designed to mislead.

Certain is opposite to:

**a**  particular

**b**  doubtful

**c**  unequal

**d**  unfailing

Answer: **b** doubtful

# WORD PLACEMENT – TESTS 7–9

Word placement tests assess several skills: spelling, grammar, punctuation and general English usage. These tests clearly gauge intelligence, as they reflect a command of English, but, like many verbal reasoning tests, they also measure an ability to focus on relevant details and to distinguish between competing information. Employers will be keen to identify those candidates possessing these skills, where those skills are particularly important.

⬤ Word placement tests are easier if you are able to prepare comprehensively. So, make a list of words and grammatical issues where your understanding may be weak. For instance, it is vital that you understand about possessive apostrophes.

○ Apostrophes to show possession where there is one owner (singular): Apostrophes are used to show ownership of something. If the owner is in the singular then the apostrophe goes after the word and then you add an s. For example:

> Tom's books (the apostrophe shows that the books belong to Tom).
>
> The rabbit's hutch (the apostrophe shows that the hutch belongs to the rabbit).

Note: 'its' does not use an apostrophe to show possession. For example:

> The dog liked its kennel.

○ Apostrophes to show possession where there is more than one owner (plural): If there is more than one owner the apostrophe goes after the s. For example:

> The girls' coats (the apostrophe shows that the coats belong to the girls).

Note: if the word is already a plural (such as 'children') then you add an apostrophe and an s. For example:

> The children's toys (the apostrophe shows that the toys belong to the children).

○ Apostrophes as a contraction: Two words can be joined by inserting an apostrophe where the letters are missed out. This is known as a contraction. For example:

> *I will* becomes *I'll*.
>
> *They are* becomes *they're*.
>
> *Would not* becomes *wouldn't*.
>
> *It is* becomes *it's*.

As an example:

○ *parliaments* means more than one parliament (e.g. 'the democracy was so weak it had four parliaments in three years')

○ *parliament's* means belonging to one parliament (e.g. 'the King worked against parliament's wishes')

○ *parliaments'* means belonging to more than one parliament (e.g. 'the people of Europe prefer to put their faith in their national parliaments' legislative abilities)

● There is no substitute for knowing the rules of English. Consider, for example, test 8 question 2:

Place the words *either* and/or *neither*:

When assessing performance, it is important to be _____ rude nor hostile. Otherwise, the result could be _____ demotivation or depression.

The answer can only be found if the rule is known: 'neither' is used with 'nor' and 'either' is used with 'or'.

There are often some general 'rules' that can help. They are not always foolproof – English is notorious for its exceptions that prove the rule. For example, words such as 'device' and 'devise' can be distinguished by the 'c' and the 's'. Often, the 'c' means the word is a noun – that is, an item (the device was useful). The 's' often means the word is a verb – that is, a doing word (to devise a plan).

● If you are unsure about the answer, think about other similar words that you do know. For example, in test 8 question 16, the difference between oral and aural can be found by remembering 'audible' begins with 'au' and is about listening, while 'oratory' begins with 'o' and is concerned with speaking.

- Notice the tense that the sentence is written in. This applies to many different types of verbal reasoning test.

- Be careful when words are so similar that the difference is difficult to know. For example, consider test 9 question 13:

  Place the word *stern* or *astern*:

  The captain told the sailor to put the cargo in the ship's _____.

  Stern *is* the rear part of the ship, while astern is *in* or *towards* the rear part of the ship. Because English is a language it is, like any language, a flowing, shifting and familiar phenomenon. However, this can obscure the fact that words do have specific, precise meanings.

# WORD SWAP AND MISSING WORDS – TESTS 10–13

Word swap and missing word tests demand attention to detail. Typically, when we read, we will get the overall meaning of the sentence, without being overly concerned about the detail. Tests have shown that even when an incorrect, even absurd, word is given, our brains will automatically correct it to what we expect it to be. This makes these tests difficult, as we are forced to override this self-correcting mechanism and identify the errors in the sentences. This obviously measures an ability to focus, to avoid distractions and to remove irrelevant information.

## Word swap

- Understand what the passage might be saying. This is easier said than done, but it may mean you need to identify powerful words that give the sentence force and character, or weaker linking words that may be in the wrong place. An ability to think laterally is also an advantage.

- Look for words and parts of speech that may interchange. Verbs, nouns and adjectives will normally replace other parts of speech that are the same. However, if the sentence is grammatically incorrect or nonsensical, then this may be because different parts of speech have been interchanged.

- Watch out for traps. One technique used by test writers is to swap words so that the sentence still forms a specific, intelligible phrase. Consider the following example:

> The essential future of management is to plan for task challenges, because change is certain to affect the business.

The sentence should read: *The essential task of management is to plan for future challenges, because change is certain to affect the business.* The two words that are swapped in this sentence are <u>future</u> and <u>task</u>. However, the phrase *future of management* still makes sense and is not obviously wrong. The only clue is when you read the whole sentence and see the word 'essential' before 'future of management'. The 'essential future' is an unusual construction, and may indicate trickery.

Verbal Reasoning Advanced Level

# Missing words

● Several specific techniques are useful, in addition to those mentioned above:

○ Be aware of the correct part of speech.

○ Know your punctuation (use of apostrophes is a particularly popular ploy that test writers can use to sow the seeds of confusion).

○ Watch for correct spellings.

○ Watch for plural tenses – and avoid misdirection. Consider the following question:

It was hard to imagine that all this devastation was _____ by one _____.

| A | B | C | D | E |
|---|---|---|---|---|
| causing | caused | caused | caused | none |
| bacteria | bacterias | bacterium | bacteria | of the above |

In this instance, bacterias is provided to suggest that the plural of bacteria is bacterias; it is not. Bacteria is already plural, the singular is bacterium. The correct answer is therefore C.

○ Look for clues about the verb tense in the rest of the sentence. Consider the following missing word question:

To overcome the problem of outdated ammunition, the army needs better _____ if the battle _____ to be successful.

| A | B | C | D | E |
|---|---|---|---|---|
| ordinance | ordnance | ordnance | ordinance | none |
| was | is | was | is | of the above |

The phrase *the army needs* identifies the verb as being in the present tense, so that rules out any options which include *was*, which is the past tense. Knowing the first part (ordnance) relies on your being able to spell, and the best way to succeed here is to read and use the dictionary.

## WORD RELATIONSHIPS – TESTS 14–16

Word relationship tests assess a candidate's ability to see links between things. First, you have to identify the exact nature of the relationship between the items in the example. Then, you have to apply this relationship to find the correct pair. This may not seem difficult. However, the questions are designed to mislead, which can cause problems for some people. An ability to avoid being misled and being able to appreciate connections are clearly important skills in today's workplace.

⬤ Think about the relationship between the words. Consider the following example:

> Disease is to pathogen as compost is to:
>
> **a**  rotten
>
> **b**  vegetate
>
> **c**  bacteria
>
> **d**  decompose
>
> Answer: **c** bacteria

In this example, pathogens *cause* disease. To find the correct word from the four choices, think about what actually causes compost to form. 'Bacteria' is the only option that can make compost.

⬤ Look out for the same part of speech. In the following example, placing the words into a sentence can help:

File is to shape as brush is to:

**a** cut

**b** hair

**c** dog

**d** paint

I can use a file to shape something.

I can use a brush to paint something.

You could not, for example, use a brush to 'hair' something.

Answer: **d** paint

Beware the options that are designed to misdirect you – which is often easy to do when the words are unusual or long.

Snow is to cold as cloud is to:

**a** subjugation

**b** geological

**c** formation

**d** water

Answer: **d** water

Again, focus on the direct relationship involved. Ice is *necessary* for snow to form. Water is necessary for clouds to form. The other options are not necessary for clouds to form.

It is the nature of the relationship that matters. It could be a component, an opposite, dependent on, causal, a result of, identical to, or something else. Obviously, things often have several possible relationships.

Consider the following example:

High temperature is to heat as sand is to:

**a**   glass

**b**   sandcastle

**c**   sand dune

**d**   erosion

Answer **d** erosion

In this example, high temperature is a result of heat. Therefore, the correct answer is 'erosion', as sand is a result of erosion. Whereas sand is a component of glass, sandcastles or sand dunes.

Be careful with words that are commonly linked. For example, in the example below an orange is often associated with a lemon and an orange is certainly a piece of fruit. However, white is used to make the colour pink, therefore, red can be the only correct answer, as red is used to make the colour orange.

Pink is to white as orange is to:

**a**   fruit

**b**   red

**c**   apple

**d**   lemon

Answer: **b** red

Notice how words may fit together. For example, tooth and brush can make one word (toothbrush) and air and plane can make one word (airplane). Brush is also a verb – to brush one's teeth. However, none of the options are verbs, so this cannot be the relationship that applies.

Tooth is to brush as air is to:

**a** plane

**b** jet engine

**c** cloud

**d** tree

Answer: **a** plane

This type of question can be made more difficult by reversing the paired words: 'port is to car as plane is to . . . air'. For example:

Port is to car as keeper is to:

**a** field

**b** bus

**c** goal

**d** bicycle

Answer: **c** goal

● Take care when faced with options that sound similar: the correct answer is likely to be the one that is specific to the relationship. For example, a triangle is one of the faces of a prism and, therefore, a circle is one of the faces of a cone. Geometry certainly describes the whole topic, while hexagonal and circular are not specific shapes – they are descriptions.

Prism is to triangle as cone is to:

**a** geometry

**b** hexagonal

**c** circle

**d** circular

Answer: **c** circle

Remember, the layout of word relationship tests may vary, but the same principle applies: they are testing the nature of the relationship between words.

## LOGIC TESTS – TESTS 17–18

Logic tests measure a candidate's ability to understand complex issues, manipulate facts and solve problems. They require a logical, reasoned approach, demonstrating precision in handling specific detail and logically inferring conclusions from the evidence given.

## Logic tests

Logic tests are sometimes referred to as *problem-solving* or *critical reasoning* tests. Logic tests are based on an ability to critically reason and understand an issue. An example of a logic problem is given below:

David and Rashid earn more than Jo. Patrick earns more than Rashid. Peter earns more than David. Who earns the least money?

**a** David

**b** Rashid

**c** Jo

**d** Peter

**e** Patrick

**Verbal Reasoning Advanced Level**

It can help to approach logic problems in one of two ways:

○ Follow the logic through in your mind, all the while keeping at the back of your mind the answer you are seeking. So, in the first sentence given in the example above, Jo earns the least. In the second sentence, because Patrick earns more than Rashid whom we already know earns more than Jo, she is still earning the least. The same reasoning is true of the last sentence.

○ An alternative approach to this type of test is to prepare this information in tabular form.

Other techniques for succeeding at logic tests include:

○ Check that you have read and understood the question, so you know exactly what you are looking for.

○ Develop the ability to quickly comprehend question stems.

○ Look out for traps.

Performance in these tests can be enhanced by:

○ Looking for the stem of the question: Each question has a central core, find this, and it becomes easier to locate the correct answer.

○ Previewing the whole question: By looking at the possible options before answering, you will know where to focus in your reading.

○ Understanding the structure of arguments: To succeed, you need to be able to break the argument down into its constituent parts. Virtually every critical reasoning stimulus is an argument with two major elements: *conclusion* (the point that is being made) and *evidence* (the support being offered for the conclusion). Viewing sentences in this way can help you to be sure that the argument is logically sustained and coherent. It is also important to be able to determine the precise function of every sentence that is given. Certain key words or phrases can help you to identify the conclusion and the evidence. Evidence is usually signalled by words such as *because, since, for, as a result of, due to.* Conclusions are usually signalled by such words as *consequently, hence, therefore, thus, clearly, so, accordingly.*

○ Paraphrasing the author's main argument: If you restate the author's ideas in your own words, this will help make the question clearer and more manageable.

○ Answering the question that is being asked: It is maddening and surprisingly common for test students to understand the point of the question completely, but then to answer the question that they thought was being asked, rather than the actual one. If the question is asking you for something specific (and it will be), then you need to ensure you provide a specific answer.

○ Reading actively, not passively: Active readers are always thinking critically, forming their reactions as they proceed and constantly questioning the validity of the author's argument.

○ Focusing on the scope of the argument: Many respondents make wrong choices because they go outside the scope of the information provided. Choices can be eliminated if they are too narrow, too broad, or simply irrelevant, put there to distract and confuse.

○ Preparing your answer: It helps when approaching each set of possible answers to have a vague idea of what the correct answer might be. As well as increasing the likelihood that you are correct, it will enable you to make the best use of your time.

○ Avoiding being philosophical: If there is a strong answer, then that is likely to be the one. It is too easy and tempting to get bogged down in possible answers and 'maybes'.

## HIDDEN SENTENCES – TESTS 19–20

Hidden sentence tests assess grammatical and stylistic awareness, as well as an ability to glean the necessary information from an unintelligible jumble of words. They also test an ability to reorganise what is often dull and confusing information into a clearly expressed and accurate form. The following guide will help you tackle this type of test. As well as the linguistic and grammatical points mentioned below for sentence correction, several other techniques are useful when tackling hidden sentences. First, look for the general direction, gist or meaning of the sentence. It may be misdirection, but it can help to give you a clue as to the correct words in the sentence. A deductive or funnelling approach is useful here. Second, recognise and question the use of powerful words that stand out, and identify words that seem incongruous or out of place. For example, in the following example, the word *castle* is out on its own: there is very little else in the sentence that typically relates to castles.

it you need out to remember that all in good link management castle depends on tiring successful personal relationships viewpoints. [12]

Answer:

You need to remember that good management depends on successful personal relationships.

Finally, check that your answer is correct. Do verb tenses agree? Do verbs agree with their subjects? Above all, are the rules of grammar, spelling and punctuation being followed, and do the informal rules (such as the use idioms) make sense and look right?

# TEXT COMPREHENSION – TEST 21

Comprehension tests always demand immense concentration and accurate understanding. They also test an ability to cope with new information given in a style that is possibly unfamiliar. These are important skills to assess in future employees and students. The following advice will help you when taking comprehension tests.

- 'Funnel' your understanding. When you approach a written comprehension exercise, remember that the first paragraph is an introductory process, bringing you up to speed with the subject, style and general topic. Next, you develop your understanding of the specific scope of the passage. Finally, you understand the author's purpose in writing the passage. This approach will help you to avoid feelings of bewilderment and will enable you to get quickly into the subject. In particular, you should look for:

○ The topic and main points of the passage.

○ The author's purpose and tone.

○ Structural key words and references.

○ Conclusions – often highlighted by heavy emotional content.

This approach will also help you develop a guide to the passage, so you know where in the text to locate the main ideas and themes.

● Search the passage for the author's views – in particular, discover the main idea of the passage. You need to relate each paragraph to the passage as a whole. This may mean avoiding facts, jargon and details. Also, you should develop the ability to distinguish opinions and interpretations from facts. Remember, the topic is more than what is said, it is what it is *about*. For example, a passage about the workings of parliament may be a technical article on the way an organisation like parliament works, or it may have something to say about the nature of democracy and the expression of ideas, or it may be both. Which is it?

● Understand the main points in each paragraph. Consider why the author included the paragraph, why he or she phrased it as they did, the progression the author had in mind when moving on to the next paragraph, and the relevance of the paragraph to the passage as a whole.

● Do not be distracted by details. Remember that the comprehension is only a test. Normally, when we read, whether it is fiction for enjoyment or texts for studying, or just news and information, we are trying to retain the information – either for enjoyment (so we can follow the story) or for some other purpose. With comprehension, memory need only be short-term so do not work at remembering it for any time longer than the last question. Also, the test writer may select a passage with flowery language or excessive detail, designed to confuse, obscure or distract. Focus on the author's message and the questions being asked.

## SENTENCE CORRECTION – TEST 22

Sentence correction tests assess your ability to use English effectively and appropriately in both written and verbal communication. An understanding of the rules of English is essential, but appropriateness of style and appreciation of how English is used is of paramount importance. The following will help you to prepare for this type of test. (Note: there are some important similarities between the techniques for answering sentence correction and those for hidden sentence tests.)

● Check that you understand the instructions. Sentence correction tests take a variety of forms, so it is vital that you do not waste precious time struggling with the directions. Typically, you will be given a sentence with

Verbal Reasoning Advanced Level

some of the words underlined. The first choice (A) repeats the original sentence, the options (B) to (E) offer four other ways of expressing the underlined section. You have to choose the best version of the sentence. So, if you think that the original sentence is best and none of the alternatives is better, you would select (A). If you feel that the original sentence contains a grammatical error or is awkward, then you would choose the alternative answer that presents the best rewrite.

Verbs must agree with their subjects. Simply put, singular subjects must have singular verbs and plural subjects have plural verbs. 'Test writers have ways of being tricky' is correct, whereas 'Test writers has ways of being tricky' is not. However, as if to emphasise their trickiness, test writers separate subjects and verbs with large amounts of text making it much harder to recognise whether the subject and verb agree. Bear this in mind if you are faced with a lengthy, wordy sentence for correction. As well as separated subjects and verbs, sentence correction questions often feature subjects that are not obviously singular or plural. For example, 'sheep' is a word that is both singular and plural.

One solution is to look out for test writers' typical tricks. These can include:

○ Phrases and clauses in commas between the subject and the verb.

○ Subjects joined by *either/or* and *neither/nor*.

○ Sentences in which the verb precedes the subject.

○ Collective nouns, such as majority or committee.

- Verb tenses must agree, and they should reflect the sequence of events. This can be accomplished if you:

○ Check the tense of all verbs.

○ Check that the sequence of events is clear.

○ Decide which tense is appropriate (it should make the sequence of events clear).

○ Avoid the 'ing' forms, as this can invariably complicate the verb tenses.

- Check that items in pairs or series agree. This is known as parallelism, and quite simply means that items should be expressed in parallel form. You should check for *lists* of items or a *series* of events, expressions such as *both* X *and* Y, *either* X *or* Y, *prefer* X *to* Y. The trick is to verify that they agree.

- A modifier should be as close as possible to the word or clause that it modifies. A modifier is a word, phrase or clause that describes another part of the sentence. Modifiers often attach themselves to the closest word, and the problem is that they sometimes appear to modify words that they actually don't! For example, consider the following sentence:

> 'I took several lessons to learn how to play badminton without getting the shuttlecock over the net'.

The way this sentence is written, it seems that the author wants to learn how *not* to hit the shuttlecock over the net! Or this one:

> 'Small and quiet, the Prime Minister's presence often goes unnoticed by those he will later command.'

In this case, it is the Prime Minister, not his presence, which is small and quiet.

The solutions are to:

○ Place a modifier as close as possible to what it modifies.

○ Be cautious of sentences beginning or ending with descriptive phrases.

○ Look out for *that/which* clauses, especially if they come at the end of a sentence.

● Check each pronoun. Pronouns should refer to specific nouns or pronouns. Pronouns should also agree in person or number, for example:

> 'It is now recognised that the dangers of nuclear war are much greater than that of conventional warfare.'

Because *dangers* is plural, this should read '. . . *those of conventional warfare.*'

Also, *it* and *they* are often misused. For example:

> 'If the team members cannot resolve their differences, the captain may have to do it.'

Here, *it* is the misused and unclear noun: there is no singular noun in the sentence for *it* to refer to. The main clause should therefore read: '. . . *the captain may have to do so*'.

● Only compare like things. The rule is that you should compare only things that can be logically compared. In other words, you cannot compare apples with oranges. Consider, for example:

'The magazine article compared the popularity of film with television.'

This is flawed: it has to be the popularity of film that is compared to *the popularity of television*, or *that of television*.

In sentence correction tests, you will find that flawed comparisons account for a significant number of errors.

Check for correct idioms. This is not a rule of grammar but a principle established in English as the right way to say things. For example:

'The pollution of the Himalayas is generally considered *(as / to be)* a major threat to the environment.'

It should be '. . . *considered a* major threat'. Although *considered to be* is also considered correct some people consider it too wordy. *Considered as* is always considered wrong.

# CHAPTER 5

## Diagnosis and further reading

This chapter provides practical hints, tips and techniques to improve performance in verbal reasoning tests.

The increasing assessment of advanced verbal reasoning skills in recruitment and training makes it essential to fully prepare for the tests, to ensure that you give yourself the best opportunity to succeed. Moreover, passing these tests is not the only reward for all your effort; many find that improving both English skills and mental agility also improve not only the quality of their work but also their approach to it.

So far, this book has given many examples of test questions, providing a great deal of practice. In addition to this, it is important to prepare in other ways for these tests. For example, the result of all your hard work practising will be reduced if you arrive for the test flustered or nervous. The following outlines some of the ways you can ensure your effort and skill are given the best opportunity to demonstrate your capabilities.

# DIAGNOSIS

Knowing how well you have done in verbal reasoning tests is hard to assess. The tests are designed to make it difficult to obtain high or full marks, so do not be disappointed if you never get high marks in tests. Moreover, you are unlikely to know exactly what the 'pass' mark is. Employers often change the target score according to how many applicants there are, the skills they are looking for in a particular job and how the other candidates have performed. For example, a score of 27 out of 40 may seem a little low, but if the other candidates only achieved 17 or fewer correct answers, this would be impressive by comparison. Also, specific jobs require specific skills. Therefore, an employer is probably looking for good performances in certain tests that are particularly relevant to the position being filled.

Despite these limitations, having a guide to standards is useful when taking practice tests. They act as a guide to highlight weak areas and to show improvement.

Score: 0–7 out of 20

Typically, if you are getting around a quarter or less of the questions right, you will need to consider more preliminary work to help you achieve the standard of English and thinking skills required for these tests.

Score 8–13 out of 20

Obtaining close to half marks suggests that you will need to address your weak areas and to continue with the practice material.

Score 14–20 out of 20

If you are able to answer more than three-quarters of the questions correctly, then your ability level is sound and, while ensuring that any weaker areas are addressed, your main task is to practise, to ensure that speed and accuracy can be sustained under exam conditions.

## Reviewing your practice test results

What matters once you have completed your practice test is to understand how you achieved your overall mark – where you succeeded and how you could improve. It is possible to improve by asking yourself not simply how many questions you completed correctly, but also how many questions you attempted during the time allowed, and how many remained unanswered. Furthermore, knowing which types of question you find most challenging can also provide a guide to areas in which you might wish to improve. So, if you answered most of the questions correctly but left too many unanswered, the solution might be to work more quickly next time. If, however, you managed to answer all the questions but too many of your responses were incorrect, then you might need to improve your technique or give a greater priority to accuracy, even though that might necessitate working more slowly.

However, it is necessary to remember that over-practising, to the point of exhaustion or anxiety, is counter-productive. Here, planning when and for how long you practise helps to maintain focus, balance and productivity.

# Monitor progress

By assessing how you are progressing, you will be able to see improvements or address setbacks quickly. It is necessary to achieve both accuracy and speed: neither can dominate the other. Repeating tests and attempting new questions will improve both aspects. Improvement is always an excellent motivator, while correcting problems quickly is a good way to avoid becoming demotivated. There is nothing to worry about when getting questions wrong; after all, an important aspect of practising is to identify your weak areas and improve your performance. If your progress declines, examine why this is happening. It could be that something is distracting you or that you are feeling pressured and low. Sometimes, a short break from studying can leave you refreshed for future work. Address the problem sooner rather than later, to enable you to get back on track and feeling positive again. Reminding yourself why this is important to you can help – being goal-oriented can sustain you through all the hard work.

# When things go wrong

When you get a few questions wrong, check the correct answer and see if you understand how to get the question right. A dictionary and a guide to grammar and English usage are essential here to improve your performance. However, always remember that full marks are rarely obtained, so do not worry unduly about a few incorrect answers. If you find that you are getting too many questions wrong – possibly less than half correct, even after some practice – you may need to develop your English skills. Highlight the questions concerned, and decide the areas of English that you need to learn. If you have difficulty with most types of question, you may wish to consider taking an English course or using an introduction to English skills textbook that covers grammar and spelling. Do not be put off. Many people have difficulty with English skills – it has often been a long time since they were taught the rules and some were poorly taught in the first place. It is important not to let past problems or general 'rustiness' stop you from achieving your goals. Of course, it will require effort and some extra time, but the problem is easily surmountable.

# SUGGESTIONS FOR FURTHER IMPROVEMENT

## Preparing for the test

Besides practising with verbal reasoning tests, what else can you do to ensure success?

Before answering this, it is important to emphasise that verbal reasoning tests are designed to measure your general ability to function in a particular language – English. The various types of test have been developed to assess your general ability, so in addition to practising the tests themselves, you can also do other things that will increase your 'word power', enhance your facility with words and language, and improve your communication skills.

Activities that will help you to achieve this include completing crosswords and other word games, and making a habit of regularly reading a variety of material (ideally written in different styles). Magazines, newspapers and different styles of books (biographies, fiction, factual) will all help you to vary your exposure to language. More than this, it is valuable to stretch and challenge yourself by reading material that you might normally avoid. Unfamiliar subjects, sentence construction, ideas, large words and jargon can all help you to develop your verbal reasoning skills. Above all, when reading, try to become an 'active' rather than a 'passive' reader. This can be accomplished by making notes as you read, highlighting the author's key points.

When you are reading, bear in mind what the author is really trying to say, the extent to which their views are clearly expressed, and whether they have made their points as well as they possibly can. How could their writing be improved? It can also be an interesting exercise to write notes or a short summary of the key points from your reading.

Reading is the most valuable preparation of all as it directly increases your facility and confidence with words and language. However, as well as reading and practising the tests, other activities you can use to enhance your verbal reasoning skills include word games, which are extremely useful. For example:

- Look up a word in the dictionary and follow one of the words used to define it by looking that up as well. See how many times you can roam through the dictionary, developing your precise understanding of words and language.

- Check words in the dictionary that you are not 100 per cent confident you understand or know how to spell correctly.

● Use the dictionary whenever you can. You will almost certainly find words whose meaning is quite different from what you thought it was – as well as additional meanings for familiar words, and words that are completely new to you.

● Find a new word each day and try to use it in normal conversation at least twice.

● Write about things that interest you. With the arrival of mobile telephony and email, writing now appears old-fashioned. It may be, but it is also fun and one way to help you succeed at verbal reasoning tests. So, start writing those letters to distant friends, keep a diary, try your hand at poetry – propose a book to a publisher if you are really feeling adventurous! They will all help your facility with language.

● Review a magazine or newspaper article, highlighting in one colour all the facts that are quoted, and marking in another colour the opinions that are expressed.

● Listen carefully to the way people speak on the radio and television, and how this fits with the other ways they are expressing themselves (through gestures, tone of voice and facial expressions, for example). Vary the type of material you listen to: from news reports to reality TV shows, films, sports events, comedies and soap operas. It is quite revealing how well – and how badly – some professional broadcasters express themselves. Again, consider what they do well, what you like and dislike about their style, how their style could be improved – and whether you could also improve by listening.

- Precis (or paraphrase) what someone else has written or said.

- Set yourself anagrams – or find a word and see how many other words you can make from it.

- Cut up printed passages of text from a newspaper, magazine or the Internet, and then reassemble them into their correct sequence.

- Using a word-processed document, ask someone to replace selected words with a space, and then read the passage inserting the missing words. The challenge is not to guess the missing word, but rather to find words that make sense when inserted into the empty spaces and make sense to anyone reading the passage.

## Performing to the best of your ability

During the tests (including the practice tests), you should:

- Remain calm and focused, avoiding panic and working systematically through all of the questions.

- Check that you understand the instructions before you begin. With verbal reasoning tests (and other types of test as well) there may be specific variations in the way you need to answer each question, as we saw in the word relationship tests, for example. So, read the instructions carefully before the test starts to make sure you understand them.

- Review the sample question, understanding exactly how the test works and which elements of your verbal reasoning skills are being assessed.

- Avoid over-confidence and casualness. Skim reading any part of the test, including the instructions, is a mistake as it increases the likelihood that you will overlook significant details or make mistakes that are easily avoidable.

- Remember that if you are unsure or get stuck on a question, move on to the next one – you can always return to unfinished questions at the end if time allows.

- Highlight 'command' words in the test instructions – those words telling you what you have to do.

- Check frequently to ensure you are answering each question in the correct space provided.

- Guessing is to be avoided, but if you are uncertain about an answer to a question, go for your best reasoned choice.

- Keep focused and concentrate as much as you can throughout the test. You have a great deal of ground to cover, so don't let up until the work is complete.

- Do not allow your mind to become distracted. Focus solely on answering each question correctly and completing the test in the time allowed.

- Leave a few minutes at the end to check your test answers.

Above all, be positive and remain confident – the fact that you are reading this is a testament to your dedication and desire to succeed, and that will take you a long way to achieving your goal. Allowing your confidence to fall or your attitude to become negative will be self-defeating, with a detrimental effect on your performance. Stay focused, positive and confident.

## Test papers

It is helpful to obtain specimen papers. This may not be possible, in which case similar papers would be a good substitute. If you do not have access to past papers, find out what will be expected of you by contacting whoever is responsible for administering them.

One of the main reasons for looking at past papers is that our minds work best when they are dealing with familiar processes. We feel more relaxed and in control of the situation. Shocks when you are sitting down with the test paper in front of you will waste your energy and interfere with your ability to concentrate. Moreover, it is helpful to tackle tests under timed conditions, as this will give you a good idea of what to expect, allows you to increase your speed and highlights any difficulties that require attention. So, familiarity is extremely useful in creating the right conditions for you to work well under pressure.

## Assistance

If possible, it is useful to discuss the tests with another person you trust, especially if they have already sat similar tests. Having this support helps you not only to maintain your commitment and sense of purpose but also to improve your results.

# Improving your English skills

The first piece of advice professional writers will give to the question 'how do I improve my communication skills?' is read more and read a variety of writing styles used for different purposes. By reading more, you will see how language works and how it is used, which will enrich your own style. When you read, learn to be critical and analytical. It is surprising how often opinion masquerades as fact. Being a critical reader will improve your mental powers and skill, while boosting your confidence. When reading, do not ignore words that you do not understand simply because you can get the gist of what is being communicated – always look them up in a dictionary. Also, being attentive to what is being said or written will improve your own listening and presentational skills.

## ON THE DAY

You must plan to arrive at the test centre in a state that is conducive to achieving your best possible score. This means being calm and focused. It is possible that you may feel nervous before the test, but you can help yourself by preparing in advance the practical details that will enable you to do well. Remember, it is unlikely that you are the only person who is feeling nervous; what is important is how you deal with your nerves! The following suggestions may help you to overcome unnecessary test-related anxiety.

**1** Know where the test centre is located, and estimate how long it will take you to get there – plan your 'setting off time'. Now plan to leave 45 minutes before your setting off time to allow for travel delays. This way, you can be more or less certain that you will arrive at the test centre in good time. If, for any reason, you think you will miss the start of the session, call the administrator to ask for instructions.

**2** Try to get a good night's sleep before the test. This is obvious advice and, realistically, it is not always possible, particularly if you are prone to nerves the night before a test. However, you can take some positive steps to help. Consider taking a hot bath before you go to bed, drinking herbal rather than caffeinated tea, and doing some exercise. Think back to what worked last time you took an exam and try to replicate the scenario.

**3** The night before the test, organise everything that you need to take with you. This includes test instructions, directions, your identification, pens, erasers, possibly your calculator (with new batteries in it), reading glasses and contact lenses.

**4** Decide what you are going to wear and have your clothes ready the night before. Be prepared for the test centre to be unusually hot or cold, and dress in layers so that you can regulate the climate yourself. If your test will be preceded or followed by an interview, make sure you dress accordingly for the interview which is likely to be a more formal event than the test itself.

**5** Eat breakfast! Even if you usually skip breakfast, you should consider that insufficient sugar levels affect your concentration and that a healthy breakfast might help you to concentrate, especially towards the end of the test when you are likely to be tired.

**6** If you know that you have specific or exceptional requirements which will require preparation on the day, be sure to inform the test administrators in advance so that they can assist you as necessary. This may include wheelchair access, the availability of the test in Braille, or a facility for those with hearing difficulties. Similarly, if you are feeling unusually unwell on the day of the test, make sure that the test administrator is aware of it.

**7** If, when you read the test instructions, there is something you don't understand, ask for clarification from the administrator. The time given to you to read the instructions may or may not be limited but, within the allowed time, you can usually ask questions. Don't assume that you have understood the instructions if, at first glance, they appear to be similar to the instructions for the practice tests.

**8** Don't read through all the questions before you start. This simply wastes time. Start with Question 1 and work swiftly and methodically through each question in order. Unless you are taking a computerised test where the level of difficulty of the next question depends on you correctly answering the previous question (such as the GMAT or GRE), don't waste time on questions that you know require a lot of time. You can return to these questions at the end if you have time left over.

**9** After you have taken the test, find out the mechanism for feedback, and approximately the number of days you will have to wait to find out your results. Ask whether there is scope for objective feedback on your performance for your future reference.

**10** Celebrate that you have finished.

Verbal Reasoning Advanced Level

# FURTHER SOURCES OF PRACTICE

In this final section, you will find a list of useful sources for all types of psychometric tests.

## Books

Barrett, J., *Test Yourself! Test Your Aptitude, Personality and Motivation, and Plan Your Career*. London: Kogan Page, 2000.

Bolles, Richard N., *The 1997 What Colour Is Your Parachute?* Berkeley, CA: Ten Speed Press, 1997.

Carter, P. and K. Russell, *Psychometric Testing: 1000 Ways to Assess Your Personality, Creativity, Intelligence and Lateral Thinking*. Chichester: John Wiley, 2001.

Chin-Lee, Cynthia, *It's Who You Know*. Toronto, ON: Pfeiffer, 1993.

Cohen, D., *How to Succeed at Psychometric Tests*. London: Sheldon Press, 1999.

Crozier, G., *Test Your Verbal Reasoning*. London: Hodder & Stoughton, 2000.

Jackson, Tom, *The Perfect Résumé*. New York: Doubleday, 1990.

Jones, S., *Psychological Testing for Managers*. London: Judy Piatkus, 1993.

Krannich, Ronald L. and Caryl Rae Krannich, *Network Your Way to Job and Career Success*. Manassa, VA: Impact Publications, 1989.

Parkinson, M., *How to Master Psychometric Tests*. London: Kogan Page, 1997.

Pelshenke, P., *How to Win at Aptitude Tests*. Kettering: Thorsons, 1993.

Smith, Heidi, *How to Pass Numerical Reasoning Tests: A Step-by-Step Guide to Learning the Basic Skills*. London: Kogan Page, 2002.

Tolley, H. and K. Thomas, *How to Pass Verbal Reasoning Tests*. London: Kogan Page, 2001.

Williams, R., *Prepare for Tests at Interview for Graduates and Managers*. Cheltenham: NFER-Nelson, 1999.

## Test publishers and suppliers

Assessment for Selection and Employment
Chiswick Centre
414 Chiswick High Road
London  W4 5TF
telephone: 0208 996 3337

Oxford Psychologists Press
Elsfield Hall
15–17 Elsfield Way
Oxford  OX2 8EP
telephone: 01865 404500

Psytech International Ltd
The Grange
Church Road
Pulloxhill
Bedfordshire  MK45 5HE
telephone: 01525 720003

Saville & Holdsworth Ltd
The Pavilion
1 Atwell Place
Thames Ditton
Surrey  KT7 0SR
telephone: 0208 398 4170

The Psychological Corporation
32 Jamestown Road
London  NW1 7BY

The Test Agency Ltd
Burgner House
4630 Kingsgate
Oxford Business Park South
Oxford  OX4 2SU
telephone: 01865 402900

## Useful websites

Websites are prone to change, but the following are correct at the time of going to press.

www.ase-solutions.co.uk

www.barcap.com/graduatecareers/barcap_test.pdf

www.bhgplc.com

www.bps

www.careerpsychologycentre.com

www.careers-uk.com

www.cipd.org.uk

www.civil-service.gov.uk/jobs/fs/fs.saq.asp

www.deloitte.co.uk/index.asp

www.englishforum

www.englishtogo

www.ets.org

www.freesat1prep.com

www.home.g2a.net

www.kogan-page.co.uk

www.mensa.org.uk

www.morrisby.co.uk

www.newmonday.co.uk

www.oneclickhr.com

www.opp.co.uk

www.pgcareers.com/apply/how/recruitment.asp

www.psychtests.com

www.psychtesting.org.uk

www.psytech.co.uk

www.pwcglobal.com/uk/eng/carinexp/undergrad/quiz.html

www.publicjobs.gov.ie/numericatest.asp

www.puzz.com

www.rinkworks.com/brainfood.maths.html

www.testagency.co.uk

www.tests-direct.com

www.thewizardofodds.xom/math/group1.html

www.workunlimited.co.uk

# Useful organisations

American Psychological Association Testing and Assessment

Association of Recognised English Language Schools (ARELS)

Australian Psychological Society

The Best Practice Club

The British Psychological Society

Canadian Psychological Society

The Chartered Institute of Marketing

The Chartered Management Institute

The Institute of Personnel and Development

Psyconsult

Singapore Psychological Society

Society for Industrial and Organisational Assessment (South Africa) (SIOPSA)

**NOTES**

**NOTES**

**NOTES**

**NOTES**

**NOTES**